Leaning into Six Sigma

Leaning into Six Sigma

A Parable of the Journey to Six Sigma and a Lean Enterprise

Barbara Wheat
Chuck Mills
Mike Carnell

McGraw-Hill

New York Chicago San Francisco Lisbon
London Madrid Mexico City Milan New Delhi
San Juan Seoul Singapore Sydney Toronto

1 2 3 4 5 6 7 8 9 0 DOC/DOC 0 9 8 7 6 5 4 3

ISBN 0-07-141432-0

This publication is designed to provide accurate and authoritative information in regard to the subject matter covered. It is sold with the understanding that neither the author nor the publisher is engaged in rendering legal, accounting, or other professional service. If legal advice or other expert assistance is required, the services of a competent professional person should be sought.

—From a Declaration of Principles jointly adopted by a Committee
of the American Bar Association and a Committee of Publishers

McGraw-Hill books are available at special quantity discounts to use as premiums and sales promotions, or for use in corporate training programs. For more information, please write to the Director of Special Sales, McGraw-Hill, 2 Penn Plaza, New York, NY 10128. Or contact your local bookstore.

 This book is printed on recycled, acid-free paper containing a minimum of 50% recycled de-inked fiber.

Contents

Foreword

*T*he Six Sigma concept and Total Cycle Time (Lean Enterprise) were two of the key initiatives undertaken by Motorola back in the mid-1980s that I was fortunate enough to be a part of. This continuous improvement methodology works, as evidenced by the fact that many companies and quality consultants are deploying it correctly. Even the worldwide organization of the American Society for Quality will be establishing a new certification exam for Six Sigma Black Belts, which truly demonstrates how institutionalized the Six Sigma process has become.

This is the type of book you want every company employee, especially executive leaders and middle managers, to read before you start your Lean/Six Sigma deployment. Everyone effects change in an organization and can relate to the various characters and their roles in this book.

The authors have done an excellent job explaining in a non-technical way the Six Sigma problem-solving methodology, MAIC (Measure, Analyze, Improve, and Control), and why it is critical that it be linked to the Five S's of Lean Enterprise.

This modern day fable, which can be read on your next short flight, depicts the "typical company" looking for a solution to chronic quality issues and a month-end delivery bottleneck, patched up with significant overtime and resulting in poor financials.

Sam is invited to visit the plant owner to help him make the decision on which machine to buy. Sam runs into a typical mess everywhere she looks in the company, including your doubting Thomas (the manufacturing supervisor, George), who has been there since the doors opened and helped the owner to build the business to what it is today.

As they work with the "problem child department team," using the Five S's and deploying MAIC problem-solving methodologies, both Sid and George come to realize the need for change—and even become strong advocates and champions for that change.

An exit strategy for Sam is developed, so that the ownership of the new problem-solving methodologies is internalized and institutionalized by the company's leadership and staff. The end comes so quickly you are left wondering what happens next.

I strongly urge anyone who is thinking of deploying the Lean/Six Sigma methodology to read this book. Based on the "real life" comments and examples used, it is evident that the authors have lived what they are preaching, successfully deploying Lean/Six Sigma in all types of applications, including manufacturing, service industries, financial institutions, government, research and design development, and aerospace.

The book captures the true spirit of Six Sigma and continuous improvement that made Motorola great and I am sure it will be appreciated by all implementing or looking to implement a Six Sigma deployment today.

—John A. Lupienski
Motorola, Inc.

Introduction

I'm "that guy."

I haven't always been that guy. It's a relatively new position for me. I joined the ranks of "those guys" only a few years ago.

You know us: we're the people your boss hires to help you address issues in your organization for which you already know the solution. Yep, that's me—one of those "damned consultant guys." I'm female, but that doesn't make a difference: "those consultant guys" are gender-neutral. So, I'm "that guy."

I know how you might feel. Someone comes into your workplace, asks a bunch of questions, and then puts your responses into a nicely packaged format and delivers to your boss a report that is a mirror image of your solution to the problem.

So, why does an organization pay for information it already has? Let's start examining this issue with a personal example of the phenomenon—me.

By the way, the name is Sam. Well, my parents, Mr. and Mrs. Micawh, named me Samantha, but that's a little fancy—especially in my world.

I work primarily in manufacturing. In fact, my informal title is "plant rat." Clients and colleagues have given me that title and I'm quite proud of it. I'm one of those very odd individuals who love the "real" problems that only a factory can provide.

So, you may be wondering, why would someone who loves the factory and "real" problems leave her job to become one of "those guys"?

I was actually very happy with my last position before becoming "that guy." I worked as part of a team to solve chronic problems in our plant. Our team was great at solving problems. In fact, finding solutions quickly became the easiest part of my job.

But here's the catch. Solving problems requires a scientific approach based on data. Since the problems were costing the company money, it would seem logical to assume that the company would provide the support required to solve the problem, right? Yeah, right!

Every step toward implementing the solution of any problem is a trial by fire. It's like making your way through a political minefield: you soon wonder why you decided to attempt it without a map showing where the mines are and how to avoid them. But luckily (or so you would think!) you live through the politics, you fix the problem, and you get the satisfaction of a job well done. Sure, you don't get a rousing rendition of "Hail the Conquering Hero" for meeting the challenge, but it feels good.

As you explain to your team that their credibility is growing throughout the organization, you wonder to yourself just how long it will take to see. But since this project was so important and the solution was so elegant, you're positive that after this victory you'll no longer have to fight political battles to solve problems.

Then it comes as a complete surprise, of course, that others throughout the organization just don't see the situation quite the same way you do.

So what do you do? Well, if you're me, you quit fighting. You walk away from that scene. I was tired of fighting for what I knew was right. I was ready to join an organization that had recognized my problem-solving skills, an organization where politics take a back seat to business decisions.

Of course, as I walked away after submitting my resignation to my boss, voices rose here and there, each a variant on one of two themes—"Don't quit now" and "You'll be sorry."

As I walked out the door for the last time, I couldn't miss the looks that were trying to tell me I was making a big mistake.

Well, I didn't think so at the time—but I wasn't so sure a few days later. As I was going through the interview process with that organization that I thought would be different, I began to realize that my ex-boss was right. No matter who you talk to, it seems there is a definite political force in any organization that can lead to poor business decisions based mainly on politics.

So, what do you do? The only thing left for me at that point was to fight the politics on my own. I decided to hang out my "Consultant" shingle.

But in joining the ranks of "those guys," I quickly realized that the profession had become contaminated. Being a consultant is almost as bad as being a lawyer, judging from the number of "bottom feeder" jokes flying around the business world.

Nevertheless, I was committed to changing things. I vowed to be the best consultant ever. There would be no shades of gray in my palette of business ethics—only black and white, good and bad, "yes, it's right" or "no, it's wrong." OK, you get the picture: there would be no "little white lies" for me.

Things went pretty well for a while. I managed to build up a strong relationship with my clients. In fact, I soon had more business than I could handle—not a bad position for a consultant. This honesty thing really works!

I could tell you a lot of stories about being a consultant, but this one's the best.

One day I get a call from my old boss. It seems the company has come up against a problem they cannot solve without me and they would like to hire me to consult.

Can you believe it? At $65K per year as an employee, I had to scratch, fight, and fend for myself. Now at $3K per day, I get hired by the same team of leaders—who are now willing to step up to any solution I propose as though it's an epiphany from above. I couldn't help but wonder, "What's wrong with this picture?"

But I know the solution to the problem and the best approach to implement the solution. Only this time, without the political constraints, I reach a conclusion in about a tenth of the time it would have taken before, when I was an employee and not a consultant. Are you surprised?

I mentioned that consultants generally get a bad rep. But sometimes it's the opposite: there's a certain mystique. In fact, I could make more money if I played the part of the guru. But, like I said, I'm committed to changing things and to being straight about it.

So, my business went along pretty well for a while, until I ran into my first big challenge as a consultant. I got a client who knew there was a problem, but didn't know what or where it was. I went through the process of determining the root cause and I planned and strategized for containing and eliminating the problem.

But the client didn't want to follow my recommendation. The top managers were not happy with the solution because it involved more cultural buy-in than the company was willing to commit to. They wanted to pay me a little more for an easy fix: "Just make this thing go away as quickly as possible."

Unfortunately, easy fixes sometimes cause more problems than they solve. There are several types of "easy fix" solutions, basically finger-in-the-dike stopgaps. You can cut costs, reorganize (again), centralize, decentralize … and all of this amounts to continuous firefighting, a continuing approach to greasing any wheel that squeaks—without taking the wheels apart to get at the causes of those annoying squeaks. You may make some short-term improvements here and there, but you know it's not enough and you can bet additional issues will arise elsewhere in the organization in the near future.

But I'm getting ahead of myself here. This book tells the story of that client, my biggest challenge—so far!

Chapter 1

SG, Inc.

A few months back, a man named Sid Glick, president of a manufacturing company called SG, Inc., phoned my office. He asked if I could have lunch with him to discuss a problem he was having at his plant.

We agreed to meet at his favorite home-cooking café. After the usual pleasantries, Sid blurted, "I called you, Ms. Micawh, because you were highly recommended by some colleagues of mine who told me that you know your stuff, that you're a plant rat who can take care of the problem."

Sid got straight to the point. I like that approach!

"Good. But please call me Sam."

"OK, Sam," he nodded, "here's my situation. SG, Inc. manufactures machine components. We can make whatever parts our customers want—gears, valves, pistons, and so on—and we do assembly. I won't bore you with details at this point. Now, here it is: I'm considering purchasing a five-axis CNC machine to the tune of $1,200,000 or a smaller, four-axis machine for $750,000."

I immediately imagined the two CNC machines side by side, with a big yellow price tag on each. (In case you're not a "plant rat" like me, I should probably explain that CNC means "computer numerically controlled," which just means that a machine tool is operated by a dedicated computer that has the capability to read computer codes and convert them into machine control and driving motor instructions.)

I listened attentively as Sid presented his situation.

"I would like you to evaluate my backlog, our part configurations, and the run rates on these machines and then help me to determine which would be the smarter buy."

He slid a file across the table to me.

It was refreshing to meet a person who had apparently done his homework. Sid had determined the root cause of his capacity problem and had narrowed his options to these two machines. I agreed to do lunch with him the following Tuesday.

I reviewed all of the materials Sid gave me, in just an hour or so. I guess I should have known it wasn't going to be that easy. But sometimes even a hardened consultant like me just wants to believe.

After we met at the restaurant, sat down, and ordered, Sid jumped right into it.

"OK, Sam, you've read all the numbers, so you know about our situation and the two machines. Now, give me your best guess—the five or the four?"

"I would rather not guess, Sid. That's just not my style."

I paused. Sid seemed to appreciate that I was candid and blunt, so I continued.

"I'd like to look at the plant and review the data that's brought you to this point. Then, when I understand why you're trying to decide between the five-axis or the four-axis, I can be sure of offering you the best advice I can give."

Our sandwiches and coffee arrived and we started eating. Sid told me he would be glad to show me through the plant. But, he explained between bites, there was no specific data prompting the decision. In fact, he pointed out, that's why he was consulting with me.

"Hmm," I thought, chewing a little more slowly. "That doesn't sound good." But I let it pass—for now. I hoped that my silence would get more out of Sid at this point than any questions. The tactic worked.

"Actually," he continued, taking a sip of coffee, "it's George who says we need a new machine." He explained that George was the plant supervisor, who had been working at SG, Inc. for 26 years.

"George says that's the only way we can reduce our backlog and start meeting delivery schedules. So," he concluded, pushing his plate to the side, "that's why I've asked you to help me decide between these two machines."

"Oops!" I thought. SG, Inc. is about to decide on a million dollar capital expenditure based on "tribal knowledge," with no data to substantiate the decision. My lunch suddenly became unsettled, so as we were at the counter paying the lunch tab, I bought some antacids.

Key Points

- It's a sign of problems when management is making decisions without specific data to support them.
- "Tribal knowledge"—although it can be a starting point in making decisions—is generally not enough in inself for smart decisions, especially since this "knowledge" may be only a belief or a feeling or simply a hope.

Chapter 2

First Impressions of the Plant

We sometimes can't see the forest for the trees.

As we drove up to the plant, my first thought was that Sid had done a good job picking out a location for his company. Instead of one single building, SG consisted of two moderately sized side-by-side structures. The two facilities were connected by a paved path with trees and shrubs planted on either side to make the walk between the two buildings more pleasant. The landscaping was nicely manicured and reminded me more of a park than a manufacturing location. The buildings were clean and the lawns were groomed professionally. In the back of my mind, I was thinking, "OK, I could spend a week or two working in this environment."

As Sid motioned me into the visitors' parking area, I caught sight of something that might have been a problem, but I decided to keep my thoughts to myself until I saw the rest of the plant. Still … in the back of my mind was this nagging thought: "Why would an organization this small need to have all those tractor trailers parked back there? There's no way they can be moving that much material in and out of this place."

As soon as we hit the front door, a small, middle-aged woman in a snappy business suit met Sid. Before I was even introduced, it became apparent that this was his secretary.

I knew I'd better make a good impression on this woman, because I've found over the past few years that plant managers and business owners think they run the place, but the secretaries and administrative assistants are the ones who really keep things going. If I wanted to do any type of business with Sid, I'd better make sure this woman liked me. In order to make sure, I slapped on my best smile and extended my hand to introduce myself.

"Hello, ma'am, my name is Sam," I said, "and who might you be?"

The no-nonsense look she gave me said she wasn't going to decide she liked me just because I smiled and took the initiative to introduce myself. Within the blink of an eye, her words confirmed what her look suggested.

"Well, I might be Joan of Arc," she said without the slightest hint of a smile, "but I am Celia Gordon. I'm Sid's executive administrative assistant."

"Damn," I thought. "That didn't go as planned." Luckily she was in a hurry and scurried away without even a whisper of goodbye.

Sid just looked at me and shrugged.

"She's always like that. Just ignore it and she'll warm up to you."

I didn't say a word; I just smiled. I wanted to tell him that it would take a bottle of acetylene and a blowtorch to warm that woman up. But, like I said, I didn't say a word. I just stood there and smiled.

Then we walked to Sid's office. There Sid introduced me to George, the manufacturing supervisor. This was the same George he had mentioned in the restaurant, who had told him to buy the new piece of equipment.

George shook my hand and said, "Pleased to meet you," and we entered Sid's office.

As we sat across the table from each other, George began telling me the history of Sid's business. It was evident that George was very proud of the fact that he was one of only a handful of people left in the company who had been there since the very beginning.

As George went through the history of SG, I realized that he had good reason to be proud. In under 30 years, the company had grown from two guys machining parts to an organization with over 500 full-time employees and more than $300 million in sales annually. They were well respected in their industry, although recent quality concerns and late delivery issues were causing problems with some of their biggest contracted customers. These problems, however, could be fixed with the new equipment. George had no doubts about that, and I certainly wasn't going to say otherwise—at least not yet.

As George wrapped up his history lesson, Sid suggested that I might like to see the facility. George was between production meetings and said he would be happy to show me the plant.

As we walked into the facility, I had mixed emotions. The consultant part of me was screaming at all the things I saw wrong and I felt an immediate urge to point everything out to George as we passed by. But the (semi) human side of me screamed that this would be wrong. Looking at him and listening as he showed me the various processes throughout the plant, I decided to listen to my human side for a change.

One thing that I couldn't be quiet about, though, was the level of negativity I sensed as we walked through the plant. As we passed, operators stared at us or just scowled. I wasn't sure which I found more unsettling.

I asked George if SG had some labor problems and he just nodded. I decided to take the issue up with Sid later, after the tour.

When the plant tour was over, George led me back to Sid's office and shook my hand at the door.

"I'm really glad you came to have a look at the place," he said. "Since Sid will have the opinion of an outsider now, I'm sure he'll listen to me."

Then George walked away. I realized that he was telling me that when I gave Sid the same recommendation as he had, Sid would buckle and get the new equipment. Whoops! This was going to be a problem, because I had no intention of advising Sid that he needed a new piece of equipment. Not yet, anyway.

As I slowly opened the door to Sid's office, I saw that he was on the phone. He motioned me to come in and have a seat. I sat down and began looking around at the plaques on the wall. Several were from suppliers for outstanding quality, cost reduction, and on-time delivery—but none of the plaques had a date less than 10 years old. Not a very good sign, but I didn't say a word about it to Sid as he hung up the phone. I just made a mental note.

"Well, waddya think?" he asked me. "Can I get by with the smaller machine or should I just bite the bullet and go all out?"

Sid spoke with such blatant pride that I almost didn't have the heart to tell him what I'd seen. Almost.

"You know, Sid, it may be possible to raise your quality and capacity levels without buying new equipment. If you would like, I can take a few minutes to give you my impressions of the facility. Then we can talk about some less expensive ways to bring your quality up and your cycle time down using the equipment you already have."

Sid smiled and said he liked the sound of that, so I asked him for a few minutes to get my thoughts together and write some notes. Sid said that was perfect, because he had a meeting scheduled that should take about an hour. He asked Celia to find me a quiet space so I could work and said he'd meet me back in his office around 4:30.

Judging by our first greeting, I expected Celia to put me somewhere in a cleaning closest filled with plenty of toxic chemicals. Instead, she showed me to a small conference room with a visitors' desk and a phone and told me where I could find the rest rooms, the snack bar, and smoking areas. A definite improvement from earlier in the day and I even thought I saw a hint of a smile as she turned to leave. But it was probably just the light playing tricks on me.

When I sat down to collect my thoughts, I realized that my impressions were even worse than I had consciously realized. Without the threat of George knocking me on my butt, the truth of what I saw came out pretty freely—and the truth was ugly. The word "ugly" stuck in my mind.

I remembered that when I got started in consulting, a friend in the business told me, "You never want to tell the customer he has an ugly baby." That was his not-so-charming way of saying that you don't bad-mouth the customers' processes or initiatives—especially when they've attempted to instill a positive improvement.

I tried to keep that in mind as I prepared my notes, but it wasn't easy. Sid had an ugly baby.

At exactly 4:30 p.m., I walked out of the conference room and headed toward Sid's office. About 20 feet from the door, George called from behind, "Hey, Sam, wait up." He jogged the few steps to catch up with me and said, "Hope you don't mind, but Sid asked me to join you."

Sid was waiting and looked eager, so I began talking as soon as we had exchanged pleasantries. Now, sensitive I'm not. If I were, I would have noticed the look on both their faces as I waded deeper into my impressions of the facility. When I was finished running down my laundry list of things that were wrong, I looked up at them and was genuinely amazed by the shocked look in their eyes.

I immediately looked down at the scribbled notes in my lap to see what I had said that would have been so devastating to the two men:

- The plant is filthy.
- There's no control of parts that don't meet specifications.
- There's no semblance of lot control for work in process or finished goods inventory.
- Operators are performing their work sloppily and to no particular standard.
- There's no apparent flow to the processes.
- There's so much inventory that no one knows what they have and what they don't have.

- There are excess and broken tooling and fixtures scattered everywhere in the plant.
- The lighting is very poor and work conditions are unsafe.
- All raw inventory is contaminated and there is no sure method of controlling inventory. Raw material is stored alongside the production lines and appears to have been there for years.
- Material handlers are running all over the plant with nothing on their forklifts, wasting gas and endangering each other and the process operators.
- Hazardous material is not stored properly.
- There are years of inventory on trailers out back. (This is what I was afraid of when I parked earlier in the day.)
- The few control charts scattered about the plant are outdated by months—but no one is even looking at them anyway, thank goodness!
- The processes are producing in batches because the setup times are so long.
- The last processes before final inspection are being starved for part assemblies for hours because of the batch and queue methods.
- People are standing all over the plant waiting for something to do.

Uh-oh, maybe I'd gone a little overboard! Sometimes I have a tendency to forget that I'm talking about someone's business when I give my impressions.

From the looks on their faces, I may have just stepped over the line. I slowly moved my chair a little closer to the door. As an afterthought, I finished my onslaught with "Look at it this way: knowing there's a problem is half the battle."

> Sometimes only people on the outside will make honest, candid assessments of a process or business.

Sid took a minute before he responded. I'm sure he was clenching and unclenching his fists under the desk.

"Sam, I'm not sure you remember why I asked you here." He

cleared his throat and continued. "I'm not looking for your opinion of the state of my company." More throat clearing. "I just wanted to know which machine I should purchase to make sure I meet my upcoming customer demands."

My response to this comment made my earlier litany look like child's play. I looked directly at him and spoke once more without my "fit for human interaction filter" in the "on" position.

"Look, Sid, if you keep up the way you're going out there today, you won't have any problems meeting your customer demands—because you won't have any customers."

Before Sid could get in his next comment, I decided to finish my thoughts.

I don't know exactly the words I used, but they were something to the extent that SG's quality had to be below one sigma with all the things they were doing wrong and that their inventory turns were a joke.

They looked puzzled. After I paused to let it sink in, I made my point. "One sigma," I explained, "means your yield is only 31%. Most company operate at between three and four sigma, which means yields around 93% to 99%."

Then I pointed out that if they wanted to compete in today's market, they were going to have to learn to be more efficient and focus on eliminating waste from all their processes, because if their manufacturing processes were bad, I had to assume that their transactional processes were in even worse shape. Of course we couldn't be sure because everything was in such disarray that we couldn't even tell how bad things were. On top of all that, the employees were so pissed off that they wouldn't tell you if the building was burning down.

George finally shook himself out of shock and said there was no way I could tell all those things from a brief 45-minute walk through the plant. He also mumbled under his breath that he should have known I'd try to dig in and get paid my daily rate forever....

Ignoring the last comment, I conceded that George might be right about my quick assessment. So I asked some basic questions:

- What are your inventory turns?
- What is your overall quality level?
- Do you measure quality as a percentage or as parts per million?
- Do you final-inspect every product you build?
- How do you determine your inventory levels?
- What does your preventive maintenance schedule look like?
- What is your operator interface? How does an operator know the state of the process?
- Are your margins on some products negative?
- Do your employees understand the concept of waste?
- When was the last employee suggestion for improvement made?
- How often do you conduct a physical inventory?
- What is the rate of over/under you typically see in inventory?

As George responded to each of my questions (usually failing to provide an answer other than "I don't know"), a look of caution began to form on Sid's face.

By the time the questions were through, Sid looked at me and said, "I've heard about that sigma stuff and inventory turns, but I don't really know much about any of it. So what should I do?"

The answer I gave really surprised Sid—and I think it pissed him off as well.

"We need to get organized out there.

"Just give me a week and I'll work with one of your teams and we'll start a program of Five S in your facility. I'll teach them what Five S means and how it applies, then work with them to establish the principles in their work area. After that, we can select some of your more dedicated people and have them teach the technique across the organization."

> Establish metrics that are meaningful for the health of your business. Metrics—measures against which current procedures and finished products can be compared—will be different for each organization. These metrics will be the goals that the company should always be working to achieve. If it matters, it will be measured.

At this George started forming a smile that grew until finally he was grinning from ear to ear.

"Yeah," he said, I'm gonna love seeing you try to get these guys to clean up their work area. There's no way in hell they'll ever do it. We can't even get them to walk to the trash can at lunch time. They just leave everything laying all over the snack bar for someone else to clean up."

George went on to explain how SG had to hire a cleanup crew to go behind every shift and pick up after the employees in order to keep the health inspector off their case.

I gave George my "I understand" nod and said, "Just give me the week and tell me where you want to start. If I fail, you pay for one week and I'll be gone. If I succeed, you may find that we can increase your capacity and margins considerably without any capital expense—and that would be a good thing."

George started to argue, but Sid held up his hand and said, "You've got a deal. Tell us which day you want to start; we'll have the training room set up and the people there for you. You have one week to make this Five S thing work. Then we'll meet with the team you're training and discuss the results."

George just shook his head and looked at the floor.

After giving Celia the date I wanted to have the first session and shaking hands with Sid and George, I walked out to the car to drive home. It was already dark outside and I had a lot of planning and thinking to do.

Key Points

- To compete in today's market, companies must learn to be more efficient and focus on eliminating waste from all their processes.
- A good way to begin a Lean Six Sigma initiative is with a program of Five S.

Chapter 3

Workplace Organization and the Five S's

O n the appointed Monday morning, I arrived at the factory ready for confrontation. In fact, I was prepared for several confrontations. I walked into the training center guided by Celia and began setting the room up for the week's training. I had planned on conducting the workshop as five eight-hour sessions, two of which would be used to actually work on making changes. I would start the class with some introductions and then head right into the training with a discussion on the identification and elimination of waste.

As the class participants—a team of workers on the main factory line—began to arrive, I realized that my planning was a joke. When the first person arrived, he plopped into his seat and simultaneously threw his clipboard across the table in front of him. I tried to shake his hand, but he just grunted and turned away. This behavior was repeated several times over the next few minutes, until I had a total of 10 sullen people sitting before me with expressions somewhere between anger and pity.

OK, so much for structured classroom interaction! There was no way I could direct these people until they said what was on their minds.

I began the session by introducing myself and telling some really lame jokes. Next, I asked each of them to take a few minutes to talk among themselves and find out something new about each of the people in the room. They started off slowly, but before too long they were talking quite candidly and grew pretty animated when they were discussing anything other than SG.

Of course, every time I tried to join the conversations, they clammed up. Being the intuitively sensitive person that I am, it took only several dozen of these false starts before I eventually got wise enough to sit on a table at the front of the room and keep my mouth shut.

After about an hour of classroom interaction, I asked if anyone needed a smoke break. More than half the class growled, "Yeah," so I told them to take 15 minutes and we'd get started.

Nearly 30 minutes later, I finally got everyone back into the room and started trying to get them to talk. My first few attempts didn't go very well. I was starting to feel pretty frustrated. Before long I was feeling sweat run down my back and I could hear my voice start to quiver.

These people were more than upset; they were downright pissed off! They weren't happy about having an outsider trying to tell them what to do.

The only woman in the group finally took pity on me and stood up to discuss what she had found out about her classmates. She introduced one young man in the class and explained to me that he was the cherry pit spitting champion of his county. It was comic, but the contribution broke the ice for the rest of the group—or at least cracked the ice *a little*.

By the end of the introductions, we were a little more relaxed, but not to the point I had hoped for. For the first half of the day, we spent more time on smoke breaks than working. But since they appeared to be as uncomfortable as I was, I decided to let it slide.

Just after lunch I noticed Sid ducking into the back of the room. I acted like I didn't see him there and hoped that no one else saw him.

I just kept moving through the beginning of my talk on quality, hoping to increase the discussion among the members of the class.

But they noticed "the suit" in the room, and they completely shut down. He just sat and shook his head. I got the impression he was thinking that he had known this wouldn't work. More importantly, I figured he was probably right.

After he left the room, the workers relaxed noticeably and I said, "Man, that sucked."

They did a double take and asked me what I was talking about. Many of the participants had no idea who Sid was because they had never met him.

I explained to them who he was and that he had asked me to help out because Sid realized that so many of their processes were awful. The participants seemed shocked to hear this.

The outgoing woman who had spoken up earlier, Michelle, said, "You mean he knows how bad things are getting here? We didn't think he had a clue."

I explained the concerns I had discussed with Sid on my first visit to the facility. I also told them he'd agreed to allow me into the facility for one week to see if we could make a difference. Last, I shared with the group my discovery that Sid was convinced that the employees would not be willing to work to make the changes.

For a split second, I was pretty sure they were about to kill me. Then they opened up in a flood of conversation. "Why should we help?" "What are we supposed to do?" "How will this help us?" And on and on .... For the rest of the day, we spent our time discussing what changes were possible and giving examples of how we could improve their processes.

I explained the seven types of waste and how to identify them in the work-

> The seven types of waste: overproduction, correction, inventory, processing, motion, conveyance, and waiting.
>
> The truly Lean organization is one that teaches its employees to be waste-conscious in all they do.

place. They spent about half an hour listing examples of each of the elements in their own work process, a total of 21 examples of areas in which they could eliminate excess from the process. I also spent some time talking about workplace organization, introducing the Five S's:

- Sifting
- Sorting
- Sweeping and Washing
- Standardizing
- Self-Discipline

Next we discussed how the Five S process would improve safety and workflow and allow them to better manage the process as a whole. We also discussed how we could reduce the costs associated with the rework caused by not controlling the process inputs.

As we went deeper into this discussion, they opened up and provided one idea after another for improving their work area. The group agreed to start the next morning's session by touring their work area and teaching me the process as it was currently performed.

In the last 15 minutes of the day, Sid ducked back into the room and listened. As the employees filed out, they passed Sid with quiet greetings and reserved smiles. Sid looked like he was in shock.

Immediately after the employees had left the room, Sid looked at me and said, "What did you do, drug those guys?" I smiled and said, "Nope. I just talked to them and, more importantly, I listened."

We started the next day's session at 7 a.m. on the factory floor. The group took about an hour to show me the process and how the work flowed through their area—or, more accurately, how the work didn't flow. As I went around reading inventory tags on the raw materials, I was surprised to see dates going back over five years. There was so much inventory it was impossible to determine what was actually needed in their process. There were spare tools and fixtures everywhere and nothing seemed to be attached to any particular area of the process.

The process was fed by work in process (WIP) from a subassembly area located across the aisle. The subassembly operators had produced so much excess inventory that they had built a "wall of inventory" around their work area. As we continued to tour the main work area, the subassembly process operators came across the aisle and asked what we were doing.

I stepped aside and allowed the operators on the main line to explain what they had learned. I was surprised to hear them repeat what I had told them during the previous afternoon. It wasn't just that they had listened to what I taught them, but that they were actually excited about what they were going to do to eliminate waste in their process.

The subassembly operators started talking about what they could do to bring their process into the main line. This move would allow them to build just what was needed to keep the main line running. The savings for this move and the reduction of WIP inventory would more than pay for the class we were holding that week, including all the resources required (*and my fees*).

It was hard to rein in the team members to the point where we could get back into the classroom. They were so revved up that they wanted to get started right away. I asked them to bear with me and we went back to the class to begin our plan for the next two days.

I started the planning session by explaining W. Edwards Deming's Plan-Do-Check-Act cycle. I pointed out the logic of the sequence: *plan* for improving a process, *do* what you've planned, *check* the results, and *act* on the results to improve the process.

I made sure the group understood the importance of *Planning*. After some discussion, they agreed that we must plan for success or we would not get the job completed. Our first step was to list everything that had to be done in the time allotted (two and a half days).

The first task in the Five S process was *Sifting*. We needed to check everything in the work area and remove everything that was not required to do the job. Next we would look at the flow of work and organize the tools and component items in such a way as to ensure safety and reduce walk and wait time in the process. The team had some excellent ideas. Once again I found myself trying to calm them down long enough to finish the planning.

Next we prepared for the *Sorting* of items. Each operator would be responsible for defining the location for his or her tools and equipment. All team members would provide their input, but for the final decision we would look to the process operator.

Last, the team would be *Sweeping and Washing* every surface in the work area and labeling all the items for semi-permanent storage. The goal of the Five S process would be to identify what was required in the work process and what, if anything, was missing—*at a glance!*

The final two S's would come with time—and effort: *Standardize* and *Self-Discipline.*

After class, my pal Michelle stayed to tell me that she hadn't seen the employees of SG this excited in over 10 years. They had apparently just given up. As the pressures of the business increased and the company grew, Sid had apparently stopped listening to all but a few of his supervisors. Subsequently the employees stopped talking to him. Before long there was a wall between the workers and the managers that neither took the time to tear down.

> There are no short-cuts to "world class." Bringing the tools of Lean Enterprise into an organization requires commitment and culture change. There is no more powerful tool in an organization than the excitement of its employees. The Five S process requires that you think in a new way about what you do at work everyday.

I caught myself smiling that evening as I drove out of the plant. I was exhausted from working to keep the group calm long enough to get everything in line for the next day, but I was excited too. It's not often that a consultant gets to break away from the managers of a company to work directly with the people who add value to the product. The experts of the process have always been and will always be the operators and no one can solve a problem faster than the people who do the work.

We started the next day even earlier, at 6 a.m. The team was dressed for work in jeans and T-shirts and they gave me a pretty hard time when I arrived wearing much the same casual outfit.

The day was long. We moved out two large dumpsters full of trash, broken tools and containers, obsolete material, and basic junk from the work area. Then we cleaned everything with degreaser. The team still wasn't satisfied. They wanted a fresh coat of paint on everything. Just about the time we were starting to put the stuff into the assigned locations, the subassembly team came over.

They wanted to talk to us again about moving their process closer to the main line. They had apparently continued their discussion after we talked the last time and had come up with some pretty good ideas. We took some measurements for their fixtures and outlined placement for the WIP on the main line. After we analyzed the proposal, everything looked like it would fit (with some minor maintenance and reworking of electricity and HVAC). We called the facility manager and asked for some help. He found a maintenance person and got the job done.

What a change the simple subassembly move turned out to be! The main line could run for over a week without the subassembly processes running. The main line would exhaust the overproduced work-in-process inventory to reduce the storage space required. This would free up the subassembly operators to help out on the main line while the operators learned the new flow, which should speed up the process by more than 25%.

We attached the hand tools used by the operators to their workbench with retractable key chains to keep the tools at work height and readily available at all times. The operators said that this low-cost fix would probably save them about 20% of their time because they wouldn't have to look for their tools throughout the shift.

By this point, so much had changed that the team decided to present the outcome of the workshop to the managers and asked me to invite them to the presentation. We had the foresight to take some before-and-after pictures so the impact was pretty impressive.

Key Points

- Use Lean Enterprise tools to identify and eliminate all seven types of waste in all aspects of the organization—overproduction, correction, inventory, processing, motion, conveyance, and waiting.

- Five S is the foundation through which an efficient organization is built.
  - Sifting
  - Sorting
  - Sweeping and Washing
  - Standardizing
  - Self-Discipline

Chapter 4

The Results of Five S Implementation

*T*he team was ready on the morning of the presentation. They had chosen to type up a list of their accomplishments over the past few days and made copies for each of the managers in attendance. They also decided to position themselves around the meeting room in such a way so that the managers were forced to sit intermingled with the operations employees to foster open communication.

When the meeting started, I took just a minute to introduce the group to the managers and the team members took over from there. As the most vocal of the group, Michelle was "volunteered" to speak for everyone. She was nervous, but her excitement provided her with the strength to get through the presentation.

Michelle started in a surprisingly challenging manner when she asked the managers, including Sid, "What the hell took you so long?" She then discussed what the team thought of the training and what they'd learned. Next, she showed the before-and-after pictures. Finally, she wrapped up by reviewing the list of accomplishments; the rest of the team chimed in where they were needed.

Five S implementation is the first step toward a successful Six Sigma integration. It gets everyone on board and excited about change and solving problems in the organization from within.

The managers asked several questions and Michelle eventually told them that it would probably be easier to go out and physically review the changes. The difference was like night and day. Everything was clean and well organized. The excess inventory was identified as waste. Excess walking and material moving had been eliminated from the process. Work in process flowed in a single-piece manner, which provided the employees with the opportunity to shut down the line when they observed a problem or had a concern about product quality.

After the tour of the process, we retreated back into the meeting room for a wrap-up discussion. Sid was first to speak. He stood up and looked at the team.

"I'm pleasantly surprised." Sid looked directly at George when he made his next comment.

"There were a lot of us in this company who really didn't believe you guys would do this. None of us thought you would accomplish as much as you have. I have a new respect for my employees and I'm embarrassed that it took an outside influence to bring this to light."

Sid went on to talk with his employees in an open and honest dialog that included answering some basic questions about the state of the business. The operators were eager to provide more improvement suggestions and the entire room agreed at the end of the meeting to continue to apply the learnings from the past week to the rest of the processes in the facility.

Sid asked me to stay and talk with him after wrapping up the meeting and he invited George to join us. We ended the discussion by agreeing that I would return the next week and we would take it one week at a time for the next month or so. Sid and George were starting to believe that we could seriously reduce costs without large capital investments.

As I left the office, Sid asked me to bring in some books on Six Sigma and Lean that I had mentioned previously so that he could begin to better understand the concepts.

Back in the car, I was glad to be going home because I was completely exhausted from my week with Sid's employees—but I was also glad to be coming back the next week. There was work to do!

Key Points

- Implementing the Five S's slowly starts the ball rolling toward Six Sigma integration. Employees get excited and upper-level managers begin to see how to change things from within.

- Dialogue between management and employees is an essential part of implementing changes in any organization.

Chapter 5

Six Sigma Strategy for Sid

*B*ack in the plant, Sid asked me to look things over and decide where I would like to conduct the next workshop. So I set up camp in the office where Celia sent me and headed out to the plant in order to find the next opportunity.

There were still many processes in the plant that needed addressing; I narrowed the list down throughout the day. I planned to make my decision first thing in the morning, but as I was finishing up for the day, I received a phone call from Sid's administrative assistant. Celia informed me that Sid wanted to see me in his office at 6 a.m. the next morning. He had a staff meeting at 10 a.m. and needed to be briefed on Six Sigma. Sid had done some research from the books I recommended and was not quite clear on the subject.

I arrived the next morning promptly at 6 a.m. and found Sid poring over a stack of books, all with "Six Sigma" strategically placed in the title. Scattered across the desk were a variety of periodicals and Internet printouts with the same type of titles. Sid looked like he was suffering from information overload. He hadn't even noticed I had walked into the room, so I said, "Good morning" and handed him a cup of coffee.

Sid looked up, took the cup of coffee, and leaned back in his chair. "So what do you know about this Six Sigma stuff?"

"In my previous job I went through the Six Sigma training. I am a certified Black Belt and Master Black Belt."

Sid nodded his head and smiled. "So you understand everything about Six Sigma?"

"Well, I don't think I really understand *everything* about Six Sigma, but I will try to help you."

Sid waved his hands across his desk at the piles of books and pages.

"I have read all this stuff and it is really difficult to determine what Six Sigma is. Some of these tell me it is a philosophy. Some say it's a quality program. All are full of statistics that are talking about things I don't really understand. It seems they all talk about saving money with some kind of connection to quality. That seems to be an oxymoron in my experience."

"Sid, there are various opinions on what Six Sigma is," I said as I leaned back in the chair and smiled. "It actually began in 1964 when Dr. Joseph Juran wrote his book *Managerial Breakthrough*. The book distinguishes between control, which is an absence of change, and breakthrough, which is change.

"Motorola initiated a Six Sigma program in 1986 and really perfected some of the techniques. A few companies, such as Texas Instruments and ABB, picked it up later, but it really came to prominence with the deployments at AlliedSignal and General Electric in the mid-'90s."

Sid shrugged and waved his hands again. "Thanks for the history lesson, but I still don't know what *it* is."

"While it seems to be different things to different companies," I admitted, "there are basic elements that are common among all the companies that have

> All leaders must spend time up front defining what Six Sigma will mean in their organization. The definitions need to be as specific as possible.

deployed Six Sigma. The program centers around using a problem-solving methodology called M-A-I-C. That stands for *Measure, Analyze, Improve,* and *Control.* Those are the four steps used in the Six Sigma problem-solving methodology. The methodology is used on chronic problems selected for Black Belts to work on."

"Wait a minute," Sid interrupted. "What is a Black Belt and where do the 'chronic problems' come from?"

"Black Belts," I said, "are people who have gone through a training process and completed projects to gain certification in the Six Sigma problem-solving methodology. The projects are selected by Champions to address chronic problems in strategic alignment with the company's business objectives."

"OK," said Sid, "so what is a Champion and where do they come from?"

"The Champions are typically selected by the Leadership Team. They are people with influence and usually some level of formal power inside the organization. In the Champion role, they are the bridge between the strategic plans of the organization and the operational level. Are you clear on everything so far?" I asked.

> The success of any Six Sigma deployment is based on how well the role of Champion is played.

Sid thought a moment. "It sounds like a pretty easy job just picking things for other people to work on. Do they do anything else?"

"The Champion role is not a full-time position," I replied. "An equally important role for a Champion is to remove barriers for the Black Belt as he or she works on the projects. The job normally takes about 20% to 30% percent of the Champion's time, so you're correct—it's not a full time job."

"So these Champions are going to spend about eight to 12 hours per week supporting a Black Belt?" Sid inquired.

"That would assume they work a 40-hour week now," I replied. "Actually how much time they have to spend dealing with barriers is up to you. The initiatives all deal with change to the organization. Remember Juran's distinction between control and breakthrough. I am sure that in your reading you've seen Six Sigma called a 'breakthrough strategy.' Accepting that definition means you're embarking on a change program."

"Gotcha," Sid interjected. "But still, what's that got to do with me?"

"Well, we said that some of the most recognized programs were at Motorola under Robert Galvin, AlliedSignal under Larry Bossidy, and GE under Jack Welch. None of these men were spectators during the program. They sent very clear messages to their organizations, messages that were visible at all levels of the organization. The message was that these leaders were solidly behind the programs and they expected every level of the organization to respond."

I paused, to let my message sink in. Then I continued.

"Leadership in absentia doesn't work when you expect serious change. Clearly defining and communicating the company's expectation belongs to the highest level of leadership in the company—and that's you."

"So," said Sid, "you mean you want me to tell everyone in the company that this is my program?"

"Exactly," I replied, "and repeatedly. That's the only way it stands a chance of working."

> Change does not happen by accident. Leaders must find a way to make the status quo uncomfortable for everyone in the company.

"OK, I got it," he said. "Isn't this the same stuff I read about in that book *The Fifth Discipline*? What was it they called it?" Sid wondered out loud. "Intrinsic and extrinsic messages?"

"Exactly. It's more than just what you *say*; it's also what you *do*. I believe there have been several books and articles that have reiterated the benefits of value-added communication. You remember the idea of management by walking around, from Tom Peters. This is the same kind of thing. Visible leadership isn't new, but it's an idea still waiting for its time."

"Alright," he said, "I'll check my schedule and see how much extra time I have. My employees will know that this comes from the top." He paused, then started up again, as if he'd just remembered something.

"You said you were a Master Black Belt. So what is that?" Sid asked.

"Some Black Belts are chosen to receive additional training after they are certified as Black Belts." I replied, "and they become Master Black Belts."

"What do they do?"

"The Master Black Belts mentor the Black Belts and train new Black Belts."

"What do all these Six Sigma consultants do, then?" Sid asked.

> The goal of a Master Black Belt should be the transfer of knowledge to the Black Belt.

I smiled at Sid's inquiry, because more people should ask this question.

"The consultants train and certify the first few waves of Black Belts. They help choose the Master Black Belts and certify them. Then, when there's a core of Master Black Belts, there really isn't any more need for consultants. Their job is to get the company to the point where they have their own stand-alone program." I paused, because I suspected what was behind his question.

"The Master Black Belts should be the exit ticket for the consultants. A *good* consulting partner," I emphasized, "will insist on developing an exit strategy from the very first day of the deployment."

"Alright," Sid said. "I think I'm getting it. We have Champions, Master Black Belts, and Black Belts who work on projects. The projects address chronic problems and projects should be strategically aligned with the objectives of the company. That about it so far?"

"Well, that and the concept of visible leadership," I reminded him.

"Oh, yeah, and visible leadership. That's my job, right?" Sid asked.

I smiled and nodded.

Key Points

- A successful Six Sigma operation begins with a clear definition of the goals of the organization's improvement process. Without this in place, the change will never be "owned" by the organization. It will always be an outsider's idea of what's best for the company.

- The Champion's role in any Six Sigma project cannot be low key: without an active, dedicated Champion, the project will fail.

- For change to occur, it needs to be known throughout the organization that the current way of doing things is not good enough. The status quo must be made to feel uncomfortable.

Chapter 6

Defining
Six Sigma

"**S**hall we continue?" I didn't want to overwhelm Sid.

"Sure," he replied. "But remember I have a staff meeting at 10."

For the next hour, I explained to Sid that, regardless of the various window dressings consulting companies hang on Six Sigma, it revolves around a basic problem-solving equation, $Y = (f) x$ or $Y = (f) x_1 + x_2 + x_3$ .... This equation defines the relationship between a dependent variable, Y, and independent variables, the x's.

> $Y = (f) x$ is the basic equation for life. You can be sure of the output only if you can control the inputs.

In other words, the output of a process is a function of the inputs. You know it's just like your mother used to tell you when you were growing up—you'll get out of it exactly what you put into it .... This simple problem-solving equation serves as a guide for the Six Sigma methodology of MAIC.

- M: Measure
- A: Analyze
- I: Improve

- C: Control

During the *Measure* phase, the project focus is the Y. Various tools—such as process mapping, basic statistics, capability studies, and measurement system analysis—are used to define and quantify the project. Besides applying the statistical tools, we also write a problem statement and a project objective and we form a team. At this time the financial impact of the problem and the potential solution to the problem are assessed. Also, members of the company's financial community must assist and concur with the assessment.

When the Measure phase is completed, we move on to the *Analyze* phase. Following the problem-solving equation, during this phase we begin to identify the various x's that are causing the Y to behave in an unacceptable manner. As we identify the various x's, hypothesis testing is used to either verify or disprove the various theories and assumptions the team has developed around the causal systems affecting the Y.

Then, after the Analysis phase comes the *Improve* phase. During this phase, regression analysis and Design of Experiments are used to identify the relationships among the x's. The x's are the independent variables in terms of the Y, but that does not mean they're independent of each other. Variables such as temperature and pressure affect each other and the interaction of the two also affects the Y. We can never completely understand the effect of an interaction without the use of Design of Experiments.

It is the complete understanding of the x's that allows us to arrive at an optimized solution to the problem at the end of the Improve phase.

Now that we have a solution to the problem, we move to the *Control* phase to institutionalize the solution. During this phase, quality tools such as mistake proofing, quality systems, and control charts are leveraged to make sure that the problem is eliminated for good.

After explaining these basics of MAIC, I glanced at my watch. It was almost 10 o'clock, so I stopped.

Sid thanked me for my time and left for his meeting. Confident that he now better understood the basics of Six Sigma, I returned to the factory to continue where I had left off the day before.

In retrospect, I've been around management long enough that I should have realized it would not be quite that simple.

Although it was a short walk back to the factory, I had barely arrived when Celia called to say that my presence was requested immediately in the executive conference room.

I hung up the phone and started back over toward the conference room.

Key Points

- $Y = (f)x$: Y is the output, the final product. The output is a *function* of the inputs (the x's). Only by controlling the inputs can you completely control the output.
- Six Sigma methodology:
  - M: Measure
  - A: Analyze
  - I: Improve
  - C: Control

Chapter 7

Implementing
Six Sigma

W hen I entered the conference room, the tension was so thick you could have cut it with a knife. How could a discussion of a data driven problem-solving program create this much emotion?

It wasn't as if it were an unproven entity. Six Sigma had been implemented all over the world. I assumed that the addition, subtraction, multiplication, and division that drove the statistics would work the same here as it did in the rest of the world. Maybe the issue was the data-driven decision-making. The gurus always feel threatened. Kind of a territorial thing, I think. Time to enter the lion's den.

> W hen bringing a new order, the best you can hope for is lukewarm support from those who were not doing well under the current structure and outright hostility from those who were doing well.

Sid motioned to a chair to his left. That probably did not give the impression of power. It could have if I would have been on the right, but it was at his end of the table. I guess it would have to do.

Sid introduced me to his staff and then spoke directly to me. "We discussed the basics of a Six Sigma program, but it seems there are a few more issues. We would like to get your expert opinion on them."

"I will try to answer any questions you have," I told him, thinking to myself that it was nice to have the president characterize my opinions as "expert," even though I wasn't sure what data he had used to determine that.

> Outlining how you will promote and support Six Sigma with the entire management team is critical to the acceptance of the deployment as it moves forward. Some will perceive any change as a threat.

Sid began the meeting by saying, "The idea of Six Sigma was initiated by our CFO, Bill Payer. Bill has read the reports about the large financial returns that many companies are reporting from using the 'breakthrough strategy.' Bill feels if it yields this level of return on investment, then we should get some of this breakthrough for our manufacturing. Ben Thair, our Vice President of Manufacturing, doesn't like the insinuation that we are wasting that much money in our factories. We have already been engaged in many improvement initiatives, such as TQM. He doesn't believe there is much opportunity remaining in our factories. What do you think?"

"First, we need to make it clear that Six Sigma has never been a manufacturing program," I explained. "Even when it was introduced at Motorola, the objective was to be Six Sigma in everything we do, which included non-manufacturing operations. GE Capital and many other financial institutions, call centers, and public utilities have all had successful deployments. The financial returns are well documented. Most legitimate Six Sigma providers require that the financial community sign off on any claims about savings. Many of the larger companies are publishing these savings in their annual reports, which are verified by major accounting firms."

I looked around the room to see if they were following me. Then I continued.

"As far as there not being any opportunities left because you have already done TQM, you have to understand there is a continuum of tools and techniques. When you reach a certain level, you have to find a way to move to the next level. It isn't an issue of who is better; it is simply choosing the correct tool for the job. Not every problem is a Six Sigma project. So, if you can fix it with TQM, then that is what you use. We couldn't buy good quality then and it still can't be bought today. Eliminating defects

> **S**ix Sigma should *not* just focus on manufacturing or operations. In order to optimize the opportunity, all *processes* should be improved with the MAIC methodology.

and waste and effecting change is a function of hard work. Period."

Sid said, "Thank you for the input. We have another issue. Our Vice President of Quality feels that Six Sigma isn't anything new; it's just the same collection of tools that have always been around. We've trained a lot of people over the years on how to use these tools already. Besides, consultants for Six Sigma charge a lot of money. You've been through the training, Sam. What do you think?"

I tried to remain calm—which was difficult because the answers seemed to me like common sense—and a waste of time. But I took a deep breath and addressed the question.

"The point of Six Sigma is not now and never was about introducing new tools," I explained. "We really don't need any new tools at this point, since the quality community rarely uses the more sophisticated ones we have. The Six Sigma methodology focuses on being able to link the tools together into a logical flow. Data is moved from one tool to another so that there is a synergy throughout the project. It's that synergy that increases the probability of problem resolution," I concluded.

I could see several nods of comprehension from around the room, so I moved on, to tackle the financial issue.

"As far as what the consultants are paid, it is a business decision, like any value proposition. Most credible Six Sigma providers have track records of verifiable results. It's not just a training program for the sake of training. A Black Belt candidate who doesn't produce results doesn't get certified."

Sid thanked me for the information and asked if there were any other questions. Nobody had any further questions. Sid told them where I was working in the factory and suggested that, if they had any other questions, they could find me through Celia. I was sure it would not be the end of this conversation.

Key Points

- Any change to the current process will be perceived as a threat by employees. The Champion needs to understand and address this issue.

- Outlining the entire Six Sigma process with every member of the management team is an essential step in a successful implementation and will result in complete understanding of the process.

- Six Sigma is for the entire organization, not solely for manufacturing or operations. Every process needs to be addressed.

Chapter 8

The Crow's Nest

I started back to the factory feeling somewhat better about Sid's understanding of Six Sigma and how it fits with his experience of Lean and how they both apply to SG, Inc. However, I knew that there were always people who needed a little more convincing.

I had barely cleared the entry door to the factory when George walked in.

"Sam, do you have a few minutes?"

"Sure," I said. "What can I help you with?"

George was looking unusually serious, so I figured, whatever it was, it deserved my undivided attention.

"Sam," he said, "before we go any further there are a couple of things I need to get off my chest." He took a deep breath.

"First, I have to tell you that when Sid told me he was going to bring you in to get a second opinion on which machine we should buy, I was *not* a happy camper. I have pretty much run this entire operation for the past 15 years and, if there was anything I was sure of, it was that I didn't need any outsider to tell me how to do my job."

He paused with an air of authority. "And second, this morning I sat in the crow's nest and watched Michelle's group for a couple of hours. I have to admit that I haven't seen that esprit de corps around here in at least 10 years. It was like we'd transplanted a whole new team of employees in that area. I also timed the process and, believe it or not, they have reduced their cycle time by over 25% in less than a week!"

He leaned forward in and smiled. He suddenly seemed years younger.

"It reminded me of the old days when we all worked as a team, when we all took pride in our product, our customers, and our company. It was fun then. If we could get that attitude throughout the plant, we could be a world-class organization."

George leaned back in his chair and sighed.

"Anyway, enough running off at the mouth for me. So, here is what I came to ask you. Remember the first day you came to the plant, I gave you a tour?"

"Of course I do, George."

George toed the floor and didn't look me in the eye.

"Well, if you have time," he said, "I would like for you to give me a tour of the plant and let's talk about what you see. I guess what I'm getting at is, if I were sitting in a crow's nest looking down at the entire plant, what would I look for? How do we make this happen everywhere in the organization?"

I told George that I would be delighted to give him my perceptions of the facility.

"Let's walk over to Receiving. We'll start there," I suggested. "While we're walking, George, let me ask you a question. You said if you could get that attitude throughout the plant, SG, Inc. could be a world-class organization, right?"

"Yes, I think we could."

I nodded and went on. "The question is, then, if all the manufacturing processes in your plant were Six Sigma, would you then be a world-class plant?"

George again nodded. "Sure," he replied. "That would mean we would only have about three defects per million opportunities, based on what you told us in the meeting on Monday. That's about as good as it gets. Nobody is perfect."

"I see." Not wanting to get into a full discussion, I said, "We'll talk about this more later. But, food for thought: if you send your perfect product to your customer two weeks late, is that a world-class organization?"

George stopped nodding and wrinkled his brow.

"Yeah, I see what you mean," he said. "But if the processes are Six Sigma, why would the product ever be late getting to the customer?"

"Let's see if we can answer that question during the tour."

We walked outside past the fleet of tractor-trailers I'd noticed on my first day and arrived at the raw material warehouse. George told me they had just completed the 10,000-square-foot building about a year ago. According to George, they had simply run out of storage space for all the material coming in.

The building looked great—except for a huge dent in the top of the tractor-trailer entry door. I leaned my head toward George and asked the obvious question, "What happened here?" (as if I didn't know).

George grinned sheepishly and, mocking the tone of an instructor, said, "We didn't design the door tall enough for the big semi's. Maybe the planning stage of this project needed a little more work."

Inside, the warehouse was ostensibly neat and orderly—"ostensibly" being the key word here. With the exception of the tractor-trailer entry aisle, there were five rows of 15-feet-high shelving running the length of the building. These shelves housed all the small parts and raw stock in cardboard boxes, with the contents written on each box. On the back wall were stacks of 4-foot by 8-foot by 6-inch plates, stacked 20 high with 4-inch square wooden blocks between them so they could be handled by forklift. All the plate stock coding (part number, P.O. number, certification number, etc.) was written on the face of the plate with a black marker. Between the front wall and the shelving were wooden pallets on which the heavier parts and pre-cut raw stock were kept.

"If Sid called you and said, 'George, we've got a hot one. We need 10 of these parts by tomorrow,' and to make those parts you needed that bottom piece of plate, how long would it take you to get that plate to the saw?"

George pondered for a moment then started calculating under his breath, "Let's see, there are 19 pieces of plate on top of it, we have to get the fork over here, each piece would take about five minutes to move …. Oh, about two hours or so."

"So, George, what do you see here? Remember our conversations about Five S and waste reduction. Think about it as though you were in a 'firefighting' mode and you needed something quickly from this warehouse. What would cause you frustration?"

George was eager to answer this question.

"That's easy. Two things in fact. First, the stuff on the shelves you can never find. Second, it sometimes takes hours to dig out the plate stock and the parts on the pallets."

"Good observations."

"Wait a minute, Sam, *you're* supposed to be giving *me* the tour. So, give me an overview of what you think could be done to make the warehouse more efficient."

I began slowly, "Without getting too detailed, here are a couple of things you might consider." I ticked them off on my fingers, one by one.

"One, you have told me you have five times the inventory needed in here. Make arrangements with your vendors to take back for credit inventory selected based on need, purchase orders, backlog, etc.

"Two, get with Purchasing and start working the rest down to a realistic level.

"Three, evaluate your vendors and then partner with select ones for better service and quality assurance.

"Four, label the shelving (row, bin, etc.) to a permanent warehouse location in your systems.

"Five, put all pallets on labeled shelves.

"Six, use plastic part boxes for small parts.

"Seven, set up vertical storage for the plate stock, using the hoist for quick retrieval."

"And," George chimed in, "with a good labeling system, we can computerize all the parts and locations. Then we'll be able to find everything even faster."

"I think you're getting the hang of it," I said. "One other thing I want to mention before we leave the warehouse. Do you see the downstream impact of two hours wasted here on the total cycle time of a delivered product?"

"Absolutely," George replied enthusiastically. "We could add several hours to the delivery to that 10-piece order, just in warehouse inefficiencies alone. But the real kicker is that the same potential for waste is at every step throughout the entire manufacturing process, from the saw, to the lathe, to … well … everything."

I nodded again. "You're absolutely right, George, but not just manufacturing. Six Sigma, Five S, workplace organization, and waste elimination apply just as well in administrative areas as in manufacturing."

George reached for the door.

"By the way, I'm also beginning to see how it's possible for our manufacturing processes to be at six sigma and not be anywhere near world class. What do you say we go back over to the plant and map out all of our processes? This is great stuff."

> Six Sigma is about quality—but not just in terms of the final product. It is quality of customer service as well as manufacturing. A perfect product delivered two weeks late is not Six Sigma.

As we walked the hundred yards or so back to the plant, George was verbally mapping out a plan to have a team address organization of the warehouse. I suggested asking someone from Purchasing to join the team so the members could become more aware of each other's unique situations and/or problems. He agreed that it was a good idea.

"We've got to get these people trained in Lean Six Sigma logic so we can start ASAP. The more people we can get working on projects and improving their work areas and processes, the quicker we transform the culture, the quicker we become more competitive and the quicker we get our deliveries back on schedule. And maybe more importantly, the quicker we get back our corporate pride."

When we walked through the back door of the plant, we walked over to a machine that George had mentioned being a particular problem in the manufacturing process.

"Ah, yes," George said, pointing to CNC machine #14. "Here's one of our problem children. This machine must have a ghost living in it. The thing will run like a Swiss watch for a while and then—bam! For no apparent reason, it spits out bad parts and suddenly we'll be days behind schedule. Our people, manufacturing reps, and anyone else who might have a suggestion has had a shot at fixing this one."

He turned to the operator.

"Joe, hand me a rag. I want to wipe off the gauges so we can see what she's running like this week."

"Joe," I asked, "do the preventive maintenance, scrap sheets, or repair records give you any indication as to what's causing the problems?"

Joe responded with a mixture of caution and pride.

"I'm the only one who runs this machine. In fact, I'm the only person who's run this machine for the past eight years. I know her like the back of my hand. I do all the maintenance, so there's no reason to keep up with that stuff. In fact, I know this machine so well I can tell when the fluids need changing just by the smell."

I couldn't believe what I was hearing. Here was a bottleneck in the production process—a machine so filthy you can't tell what color it is. There were jigs, tools, old die parts, scrapped parts, oily rags, old gloves, magazines, and mounds of chips covering the thing, and even an old chair next to it for the machine operator. And, as one would expect, there was a small mountain of incoming material on one side of machine #14 and the next process is sitting idle waiting for parts.

George gave me that perplexed look again.

"You know, Sam, something just dawned on me. We've just proved that we can eliminate waste in the warehouse through Five S and workplace organization and the warehouse is going to be more efficient, but if I get the material over here and it just sits waiting for machine #14 to start working, have I really gained anything?"

"Good question! Let's go to your office and talk about that crow's nest overview."

When we got to George's office, we both got a cup of coffee. I noticed that George had copies of some of the periodicals and Internet printouts that I'd seen on Sid's desk. Good, I thought. Then I launched right into an answer to his question about the gains realized by getting raw material to a bottleneck process sooner.

"OK, here's the situation. The reason SG, Inc. is still in business is that you're providing a product somebody is willing to pay you to make. Right?"

George nodded.

"But, over the past couple of decades there have been significant changes, such as technological innovations, information access, new international players, etc., so it's more and more difficult to remain profitable and stay in business."

He nodded again.

"Not long ago, the formula for determining the price to charge for a product was simple: $P = C + M$. You determined how much it cost to make, you added the margin you required, and that was the price. Today, largely as a result of communication intelligence, customers are smarter and better informed, with options they never had before. To remain competitive, you've had to change the formula. Today's customer has a large influence on the price, so we've got to salvage an acceptable margin by eliminating costs by being smarter and more efficient."

I was on a roll, so I continued.

"That's where Lean and Six Sigma come in. Lean addresses continuous improvement, Five S, waste identification and elimination, workplace organization, vendor relationships, visual factories, error proofing, process standardization, culture changes, physical arrangement of the facility.... All of that promotes and ensures an efficient, synchronous flow of products and information throughout the organization."

I paused, to let George absorb it.

"Lean eliminates 'noise' and establishes a standard. Six Sigma and its tools are used to resolve any negative deviations from that standard. So with the complement of Lean and Six Sigma, the proverbial *bar* is perpetually raised."

> Lean allows the accessible variation in the process to surface so that we can work on more difficult variation issues from a statistical perspective.

"So," George said, "what you're saying is, on machine #14, for example, clean up that mess down there, Lean that process, get rid of what you're calling 'noise,' and then we can use the Six Sigma tools to deal with variation and finally get to the root cause of our quality problems."

I was glad to see how quickly George picked up on the possibilities.

"There's a little more to it than that, but yes, that's basically it. Remember the formula $Y = (f) x_1 + x_2 + x_3$ .... If you want the Y to perform within a specific acceptable range, you've got to identify and control the x variables."

The phone rang. George answered. It was Sid. After a short conversation and a little profanity, George hung up.

"Sorry, Sam, but we're going to have to put all this on hold until after the first of the month. Here it is the 25th and it doesn't look like we're going to make our numbers this month. Sid's on a rampage and wants to do some rescheduling. He wants me to shut down Michelle's line this afternoon, retool it, and pull some purchase orders from next month so we can book them. You know how it is."

He sighed.

"Let's see … Monday is the 2nd. Call me then and we'll get started again. Things are usually pretty quiet the first couple of weeks of the month. Maybe we can get going then."

I got up and left his office without saying a word.

Key Points

- Lean and Six Sigma are for any process in the organization, not just for manufacturing. To be a Lean Six Sigma company, managers must address all processes, from the factory floor to customer service.

- Lean establishes the standard. Six Sigma removes the deviations from that standard.

Chapter 9

A New Commitment

As I walked away from my conversation and tour through the plant with George, I couldn't help shaking my head. All the talk and all the eye-opening conversations still hadn't changed Sid and George's approach to managing the business. It was still just project work. It was still firefighting to get the numbers.

I walked by Michelle's operation as I headed toward the front office. She yelled at me from across the aisle. As I approached her station, she asked, "Who let the air out of your tires?"

I started to explain what had just occurred with George. She held up her hand.

"Don't give up on us," she advised. "Just keep working with George; he'll get it eventually. We all think that George is a smart guy and he wants to make things better. You just have to give him some time to understand."

She was right, and I knew it. I couldn't give up on George quite yet. I left the warehouse and headed for Celia's office.

"Ms. Gordon, would you mind scheduling the large conference room for George and me tomorrow?"

Once again Celia caught me off guard with her response.

"Oh, please, Sam, call me Celia. With all the wonderful things I've been hearing about the work you are doing around here, I'm happy to help you out."

Later that day, I made sure I just happened to be leaving the facility as George was walking out the door. I walked over to him and asked for a minute or two of his time. He said he was on his way to grab a sandwich and a beer and invited me to join him.

"Beats the heck out of room service," I replied.

He nodded and we walked out to our cars. He shouted over his shoulder, "Just follow me" and got into his car.

I followed George off the plant property and out to the country, where the blacktop turned into a lightly graveled dirt road. The setting was beautiful. The bar was tucked under a stand of trees that bordered a small but quickly moving river.

I took a deep breath of the clean air and laughed as we walked toward the bar. He grinned as usual and said, "You won't be sorry."

We walked in and sat on two of the mismatched chairs. George shouted out an order of two beers and two Cuban sandwiches. Then, he turned back to me and said, "Remember, you trust me."

We started shelling peanuts and dropping the shells on the dirt floor while the owner made the sandwiches behind the bar.

I started the conversation head on.

"I've been thinking about our talk this morning, George. Something has been eating at me all day and I just want to talk with you about it. Did you notice that, even after we reviewed all the process issues in the facility, your last word in the discussion was that you had to fight fires again at the end of this month?"

I stopped short of asking what was wrong with him, because Michelle was right: this guy was not dumb. The expression on his face told me he'd already been thinking of this very issue. I hoped that he was ready to talk about breaking the vicious circle of practices and habits he was using to manage the business.

George popped another peanut into his mouth and said, "You know, I've been thinking about that too. We need to break this reliance on firefighting and fix what's broken or we won't get anywhere."

I was relieved to hear him say that. I was about to encourage him to continue when the bar owner brought the Cubans and the beers. All conversation halted as I took my first bite of the sandwich.

"Oh, my gosh!" I exclaimed with my mouth full. "This has got to be the best Cuban sandwich I have ever tasted! How did you ever find this place?"

George explained between bites that the owner, Gloria, had been his fifth grade teacher and this bar was her retirement plan. He spent as much time in the place as possible to help supplement her income. George also explained that he made it his business to bring in as many people as possible to introduce them to the great ambiance of her fine establishment.

"Well, you've got me hooked," I said, swallowing another delicious bite. "She can count on my business as least once a week as long as I'm working with SG!"

George and I laughed as he yelled the good news across the bar to Gloria. She said she wasn't surprised and brought us another pair of Coronas without asking. This was somebody who knew how to satisfy her customers—not to mention how to promote her bar. There's nothing wrong with being a good businessperson.

As we finished our sandwiches, George and I also finished pulling together a plan of attack for breaking his fire-fighting mode and tackling the organizational issues directly at the root.

We parted ways with the decision to meet in the large conference room at the plant first thing the next morning. I didn't tell George that I had already reserved the room.

Key Points

- It takes intelligence to understand the advantages of Lean and Six Sigma. It takes courage and good leadership to take action on that understanding.

- If managers put improvements on hold so they can fight fires, they can be sure that there will always be fires to fight.

Chapter 10

Lean: Listening to the Process

Georg was surprised when he walked into the conference room the next morning. I was already making notes on the whiteboard and all the members of Michelle's work team were sitting around the large conference table.

I had written in large bold letters at the top of the board:

Balancing Work Flow

As George took his seat, the chatter in the room died down and we began the meeting. I started off by explaining that the crow's-nest view made it evident that Michelle's process was still the bottleneck. Despite the obvious issues surrounding CNC machine #14 that George and I had looked at on our tour of the plant, we had to prioritize projects. Michelle and her team were already involved in the Six Sigma implementation and training and the problems they had on the main line were more important than the single CNC machine. We had to find a way to eliminate the capacity issue and free up some extra time so that Michelle's team could run in sync with the rest of the plant.

I was starting to facilitate a brainstorming session when Michelle stood up and suggested that we move to the factory floor. Everyone thought that was an excellent idea, so we picked up our flipchart and walked out to the process. The night shift had agreed to stay over an hour to continue the process while we conducted the meeting and they were hard at work when we walked up to the line.

The Five S and Visual Factory work completed earlier by the team made it very easy to see the flow of the process. Material and quality issues were readily apparent just by watching the process in action. When the team members began brainstorming, the ideas came faster than I could add them to the list.

"Whoa!" I shouted. "I can't keep up with you guys! Slow down! Or, better yet, who wants to take over as scribe for this session?"

George didn't really volunteer; he just took the pen from me and started writing. While relieving my hand cramp, I had the opportunity to watch the process for a while. I turned to George and said, "Add 'rework' to the list."

George started to write down rework, but Michelle stopped him. In fact, all of the members turned around and looked at me like I was crazy.

Bob, one of the newer employees on the line, spoke up.

"What are you talking about? We don't have any rework on this line. Our first-time yield on this process is over 98%."

I held my hands up to stop Bob from going on.

"Wait, wait, wait! I'm not trying to insinuate that you guys are doing a poor job. I just want to make sure we capture all the opportunities available to us."

Michelle spoke up next.

"Well, what are you talking about then, Sam? We don't see any defects on the line, the scrap bins are empty, and there's nothing piling up for quality inspection."

I couldn't argue. The team had done a great job of setting up a visual workplace. A casual observation would not reveal any problems.

I walked toward one of the workstations and addressed all of the team members.

"Well, let's talk about the tools you're using to complete the tasks at this process."

I turned toward George and said, "George, flip the page on the chart and let's list all the tools we are using for each station."

> Watching the process will allow you to see waste in the system. You cannot find the problems from a computer terminal or an office. Look for things that are not required for the value added activities of the tasks being performed.

George began writing as we dictated a complete list of all of the tools being used in the process:

1. impact wrenches
2. rubber mallet
3. square
4. drill for reaming
5. tap
6. hoist

As we finished the list, the class turned back to me and Bob asked again, "OK Sam, where is the rework?"

I started to explain, but then one of the operators gasped.

"It's the reamer," she said. "We are using the reamer on every unit!"

Michelle shook her head.

"It can't be the reamer. We can't build parts without it, so the reamer is not rework—it's part of the job."

I prompted Michelle for more information about the process and, in particular, exactly what caused them to ream every unit of production. As I spoke, I started timing the reaming process. Michelle spent the next several minutes explaining the process to me.

"I've been working on this line for more than 20 years, Sam, and we've always reamed these holes. You can't expect to join three pieces of metal together in multiple locations without reaming the holes so that bolts can fit through them."

She smiled patiently and went on to explain.

"If we don't ream the holes, the unit won't be square and the components down the line won't fit properly. So," she concluded with a smile, "reaming isn't rework; it's just part of the process."

"Well, Michelle," I explained, "while you were talking just now, I timed three cycles of production. Reaming multiple holes adds over five minutes to the total cycle time for your process."

I didn't want to push too hard, but I needed to make sure that she understood where I was trying to lead her.

"What if the holes lined up perfectly when the parts were stamped? Would you still have to ream them?"

While Michelle thought about my question, Bob spoke up.

"Of course you wouldn't have to ream anything. But if you think you could ever stamp those holes that perfectly, well, you're nuts!"

> Often, improvement opportunities are pushed aside as being impossible before they are fully investigated because the historic knowledge of the organization will not accept the possibility.

His coworkers paused a second and then let out a loud laugh.

I knew it was important to pursue the point while they were still laughing.

"OK, OK," I smiled, "but if we could stamp the parts perfectly, that would eliminate the reaming process, right?"

They all continued to snicker, but Michelle nodded. I pressed on.

"So if we could eliminate the reaming process, would our cycle time balance out better with the main line?"

George had been pretty quiet up to this point, but he finally spoke up.

"If we could drop the reaming process, we would be able to eliminate all the overtime from this process and still work slightly faster than the main line."

He paused a second.

"But I have to agree with the team on this one, Sam. I don't think it can be done."

He went on to explain that they had looked at the stamping process a couple of times. The equipment was in good shape and the engineering group couldn't find any problems with the program.

We didn't notice, but Sid had walked up behind us and was listening to the discussion. After George finished explaining why the reaming process couldn't be eliminated, I asked him to have the engineer and the press operator paged to the stamping building so we could have a look at the process.

George looked skeptical, but he had the two men paged as I'd requested. Michelle said I was crazy and started rounding up her team members so they could get back on their process. As I walked over to the stamping building, I was wondering if I had lost my mind, as everybody seemed to believe.

At 11 that evening, I walked out of the plant and shook the hands of the two men who had stayed with me to look at the process for more than 14 hours. I was just about to get into my car when I heard someone call my name from across the parking lot.

"Sam! Hey, Sam, wait up!"

I turned to see George and Sid running toward me.

"We couldn't leave while you were working out there all night," George said, "but we didn't want to interrupt."

"I stopped by a couple of times to see how things were going," Sid said, "but you three were huddled so tightly that I figured I'd just let you go at it."

I was surprised to see the two of them hanging around there that late, but I was happy that they were interested enough to wait to see what we'd found out.

"Well, I didn't figure it out. We looked at everything—the program, the specification, the equipment. Everything was within the tolerance limits defined by the design engineers and we couldn't find a reason for the misalignment. We were frustrated."

I paused as George and Sid nodded knowingly. Then I continued.

Brian, the engineer, looked at the program for most of the night but couldn't find any fault in the logic. Jason, the press operator, showed me the dies and the setup tools he used and we couldn't find anything wrong there either.

Then, around 9 p.m., we all sat down for some coffee. I asked Jason to tell me what had been done on the process over the past 20 years.

Jason explained that he'd been running the process since it was started. He reached into his back pocket and pulling out a small notebook. What a surprise! He had kept process notes on everything that had been done since the beginning.

I asked if I could take a quick look at his notes. They were particularly well laid out and very complete. I didn't see anything that would lead me to believe that the process had been disrupted in any way.

I picked up my cup and finished my coffee. A strange look came over Jason's face.

"You know," he started slowly, "there was one thing. It's probably not really important, but when we were setting up the process, we couldn't be sure which side of the die was supposed to be facing up. The process supervisor came out with the engineering team and measured the die and all the locator pins and they decided that the die was symmetric. The engineers said that since the die was equal on all sides it didn't really matter which side faced up. We marked the die so we could be sure we always do it exactly the same way—and that's how we've been doing it each time we set up the machine."

I looked at Jason and he read my mind. We ran back to set up the machine and run parts, not wanting to wait until the next day to check our theory.

After turning the die over and setting up on the opposite side of standard, we stamped enough parts for one unit of production in the assembly process and had the parts moved to the main line for a trial run.

Michelle's team—the morning shift—was long gone, of course, but the third shift team was more than happy to help. We threaded in the unit we had just stamped and, as they laid the parts on the fixture, Jason, Brian, and I held our breath.

One of the operators—a nice guy named Marty—came over with the reamer, but I stepped up just as he was moving into position.

> **I**f employees are not trained to identify waste, they will adopt non-value-added activities, such as rework, as part of the process—even going so far as to write the steps of rework into their standard process documents.

"Could you try bolting it up without reaming?" I asked.

He looked at me and shrugged.

"Sure, but I've been doing this for over five years and I've never seen a frame go together without reaming. I don't see why it would start working right now."

Marty was kind enough to humor me. He handed his coworkers the bolts for the frame. They positioned the frame on the fixture—and the bolts slipped easily into the holes. Their mouths dropped open and all eyes shifted to me.

Sid and George reacted the same way as I got to this point in my story. I recognized it in their puzzled expressions.

"Sam," George started slowly, "I thought you said you didn't figure out what was wrong with the process."

I smiled.

"Not I. It wasn't I who figured it out. It was Jason, when he remembered the problem and when it had started. His notes and his memory allowed us to fix the problem."

I opened my car door and turned to Sid.

"You have a lot of great people in this company, Sid. Make sure you take advantage of their willingness to offer suggestions for improvement."

I said good night and drove away. It had been a long day. But I couldn't help smiling ... because I love this job!

Key Points

- Examining the entire operation from the "crow's nest" will allow you to find the problems in the system.

- Oftentimes, the problems have become so imbedded in the process that they aren't even realized as waste. If an organization is to achieve six sigma, employees must be trained to look for waste in every aspect of their jobs.

Chapter 11

Full Circle: Lean to Six Sigma to Lean to Six Sigma

I received a phone call from George one morning a few weeks after we'd corrected the stamping process. His voice sounded a little odd.

"Sam? George here. Hey, could you stop by my office sometime this morning?" He paused and cleared his throat. "Yeah, we've got a little situation here."

I soon found out that George believed he'd found a process where using Lean, Six Sigma, or a combination of the two wouldn't solve his problem. He wanted help.

He was more frustrated than I'd seen him since my first days in the plant. He'd seen enough of the various projects to recognize the potential of Lean and Six Sigma. He'd even hit the level where he supported the two programs publicly.

George was getting faith. He had not hit the religious level yet—and now, unfortunately, here was a situation where it seemed it would not work. His faith was shaken and I'm sure he was concerned about the public stand he had taken. From my purely selfish standpoint, I was not ready to lose his support and commitment to the program and the methodology. I just could not allow him any reason to change his mind. It was critical that I find a way to prove to him that the tools would not let him down.

George explained that there was a subassembly process in which some compounds were mixed to form a rubberized compound that was used later in many of their products. Because this compound was formulated off the main line, it was considered a subassembly process. One of the key issues with this process was that it ran slower than the production line. Even though it was not part of the main line, it was the bottleneck because all other processes were controlled by the availability of material from this subassembly process.

"Fortunately," George concluded with a slight, wry smile, "this hasn't been a big problem so far—but that's just because we've been running overtime each day and on weekends to make up the shortages."

Realizing that this process was critical to the success of the facility, he had selected it early on as a project for the Lean classes. The operators on the line had gone through the Five S and Standardized Work classes and reduced some of the queue on the main line, but it was still a bottleneck.

Next, they had targeted the process for optimization with the Six Sigma tools, but they still didn't get enough extra capacity to eliminate the queue.

Finally, after all the recommendations from the Six Sigma program had been implemented, George had had the team do the Five S and Standardized Work again, since the process had changed.

"I really believed," he explained with a sigh, "that all this work would improve capacity enough to eliminate the queue. But the mixing process is still too slow." He muttered an expletive under his breath. "Sam, I just have no idea what to do next."

After a short discussion, I found out that the mixer they were using was an older unit and that, due to normal use and wear, it had lost some of its inherent capability.

There was another mixer in the plant. The second mixer was

newer, but when the team had attempted to mix this formulation on the newer mixer, they were unable to produce a compound that met specification. They had run some long-term capability studies and found it had a capability index Cpk of just over 0.33—one standard deviation from the closest specification limit. In other words, the process was only at one sigma.

George had not figured out all of the statistics, but he had checked around, so he knew how bad it was. By convention, a Cpk of less than one means a process is incapable of generating a product within specification limits. In contrast, the Cpk for a six sigma process is 1.5 or greater.

George knew, then, that the new mixer, with its Cpk just over 0.33, would be far from good enough.

George and his supervisors had made the strategic decision to stay with the old mixer and the queue rather than use the new mixer and try to figure out how to separate the good material from the bad. They also figured out that any extra capacity they gained would be lost while material piled up in front of the inspection process, not to mention what they lost to scrap.

I didn't want to make George feel any worse by trying to enlighten him to the fact that 100% inspection is not inspection, but sorting. So I bit my tongue and then started asking questions.

"Do you really think the issue is trying to squeeze extra capacity out of this machine or is the problem really the inherent capability?" Before he answered, I asked a follow-up.

"Would it be easier to take a machine that has the ability to produce an adequate amount of material and focus on improving the capability?"

George replied as I hoped he would.

"I never really thought of it that way." He paused, then explained, "We usually just do inspection."

As I approached the mixer, it was apparent that the Five S fairy had dropped by. Things were clean, organized, and labeled. Good start. Some of the noise was out of the system. Processes were documented. It looked like George was serious about the Five S and Work Standardization. It wasn't my program any more: it appeared he had taken over ownership. I was impressed.

The work that had been done was a good first step toward institutionalizing the two initiatives and making them the process for solving chronic organizational issues. When the improvement process transitioned to the way SG did business, we would really be making progress.

I knew I could probably solve the mixer problem within a few days by myself, but then it would be my solution. In order for this process to be meaningful, I needed to make the solution belong to George and his team. They had to walk away from the situation believing that next time something like this surfaced they would be equipped to handle it—successfully.

Before getting too deep with all the players as a team, I wanted to get up to speed on the process. I began with the older mixer. I drew a simple process map on a piece of paper, blocked out the steps, and identified the various materials.

> Consultants cannot solve Six Sigma Projects for the organization. Members of the organization must solve the problems for themselves with the consultants' help. That is the only way that true change can occur in the organization.

The tools and materials were sitting around the machine as inputs. I also took some time to review the other documents and controls, which were easily accessible. The process map I sketched wasn't a thing of beauty with all the correct symbols and notations, but it was accurate.

By completing this rough, high-level map, I could introduce it at the first team meeting to help focus the group.

In a more traditional Black Belt project, such as I'd worked on in the past, we would have taken the time to complete this task in a conference room with the team. But involving everyone in the operation tended to be a longer process, followed by hours on the computer to make it "look pretty."

> **I**f the project problem is chronic and important to the organization, the Champion should have no problem supporting the Black Belt in solving it. If the problem is not worth the time, then the wrong problem has been chosen.

Maybe that was where the idea came from that Black Belt projects take four to five months. Sure, the certification process took that long, but after certification the projects should be completed much more quickly.

After capturing on my map all of the steps I could observe, I started a conversation with the mixer operator, Doc. He'd been keeping an eye on me since my arrival. Now was the time to involve him.

"Hey, Doc. Do you have a moment? I'd like your opinion on something I'm doing here."

I showed him the pages I was working on and began explaining what I'd been drawing. He studied the drawing carefully.

"My opinion is that you should definitely not give up your day job to go into art." He smiled slyly.

"And that was my big dream!" I laughed. "But you know what I mean, Doc. Do you think that my map represents all of the steps here?"

He studied the drawing for a few moments and pointed out a few things I had missed.

Then we talked about what George had asked me to do. Doc said it made sense to him, but that he knew for a fact that the newer mixer couldn't make the material correctly. I asked him if he had any idea why.

Well, I've made suggestions from time to time, you know. I know my mixers." He looked over at the machine. "But I'm just an operator, so nobody paid any attention to me. So, I figured … why bother?"

I thanked him for his input and asked if he would be interested in being part of the team to work out how to move the material to the new mixer.

Doc said he couldn't understand why I would ask him, since the others had ignored him, but he'd been talking with Michelle about what we'd done on her line and he would give it a try. I told him I was interested in his input, since I really didn't know much about mixers and it would be good to have someone with his years of experience to help me out.

I wanted to tap into his memory of all the things that had been done in the past. Tribal knowledge can be dangerous when taken in large doses, but it can also be valuable in determining where to go next, because it helps you better understand where you've been.

I returned to my makeshift conference room/office to begin listing categories of potential team members.

George was listed as the process stakeholder, since he would be the beneficiary of the project. The process supervisor would be a stakeholder also. I knew there were some positions that had to be represented: an off-shift operator, the process engineer (since it was their process), someone in maintenance, and someone in materials. These were the "have to have" people. I would add the politically correct ones later.

Next, I headed to George's office to get some help with names. He was way ahead of me: he had already begun listing potential team members. He gave me the names of the people he considered best qualified for this project and I returned to my work area. As I looked at the list, I decided it was a good starting point.

The first order of business was a little politicking. I was headed for the supervisor's office so I could meet him and let him know what George had asked me to do. When I was done there, I would see the process engineer for more of the same.

The next day, we held our first team meeting. I had drawn my process map on the board prior to beginning the session, so I let the team members interact and I took notes.

The process engineer and the rep from materials explained why what was drawn on the map wasn't the way they set up the process. The operators explained why what the engineers set up didn't work. They all used lots of phrases like "I think …" and "I feel …" but presented no data. Nobody even offered to go get some data. The notes I was taking on the process "as is" versus the process "as planned" would come in handy when we began to develop hypotheses about the possible causes.

The team adjourned the meeting after assigning action items for several members. Our first order of business was to gather enough data to run a capability study. The entire team agreed that the most critical issue was to start the measurement system analysis (MSA).

Since all of our solutions would be based on data from the process, it was important to believe in the data we collected. The discussion about MSA generated the typical response. The quality department and the process operators angrily explained that they had a calibration program.

So, we ran through the usual story about how calibration was a measure of gage accuracy—and not even a complete picture of all of that. Knowing the gage is capable of measuring correctly does not ensure that it is being used correctly to collect accurate information about our process. Gage repeatability and reproducibility (GR&R) determines precision. Measurement system analysis must include both calibration and GR&R.

Through all the projects I had worked in the past, I knew that the process map and the MSA were two things we couldn't do without. I explained to George (who was growing impatient) and to the team that these tools were not optional. The tools lead to the solution. Without using them in the correct order, we could be scrambling for the answer for weeks or even months without ever finding an acceptable solution.

During the next few days, we completed the process map, problem statement, objective, and capability study.

Then, once we had documented the process in our map, determined our objective, and ensured through the MSA that we would be collecting accurate information about every part of our process, we then collected data.

We fed all that data into a document called a Failure Modes and Effects Analysis (FMEA). I explained how the FMEA software uses the product of three values—occurrence (capability study), detection (measurement system analysis), and severity (test, reliability, and field failure data), rated on a 1 to 10 scale—to produce a risk priority number (RPN) for each potential failure. The RPNs can be used to perform a Pareto analysis and set priorities for the Analyze phase.

Several members of the team asked why we were going to all that trouble when there are various voting methodologies used in other problem-solving techniques, so I took a moment to explain that the FMEA is the only tool that attempts to remove some of the subjectivity and synthesize the various inputs to provide an analysis with a higher-level view of the process.

> The first steps in tackling a Six Sigma Process are the process map, problem statement, objective, and capability study. Without these essential foundations in place, the project cannot succeed.

We were progressing through the Six Sigma tools when we received some bad news about the MSA. The elongation testing had an unacceptable score. In many situations, this stops all progress on the project because it means that our data is suspect. This bad news had one benefit: I was somewhat relieved, when I noticed their looks of frustration, to realize that the team members understood the importance of the MSA.

We did not have the time to hold up the project while we fixed the gage, nor did we have the financial resources to order a new gage and retrain all the operators in the methodology of measuring our product. We made the decision to run multiple samples and use the averages of the samples for the gage reading.

I pointed out to the team that this method of measurement reduces the standard error of the mean by taking the square root of the sample size (n) as the denominator. I made sure that they realized that the solution wasn't good for production, but it could be used to keep the project moving.

Our temporary solution allowed us to get the project back on track. The team didn't pretend to understand all the statistics, but they were comfortable enough with the explanation to move forward.

As I guided the team to the Analyze phase of the project, we had set up various parameters for testing. We knew there were some interactions among the various compounds. After all, interactions are the reason for mixing in a chemical process. Hypothesis testing is not a good tool to evaluate those process parameters.

The team and some managers outside the project also had theories about various suppliers that needed to be evaluated. This didn't surprise me; the supplier issue always comes up. After all, it's usually much easier to point the finger at the supplier than to fix your own process. The supplier rarely proves to be the root cause, but you still have to examine the possibility just as seriously as any other. So, the team asked the supplier quality group to look into the suggested issues while we continued to focus on the internal capability problem.

We set up the tests and collected data from the process, taking care not to inflate sample sizes. Large sample sizes force the test to be too sensitive and this excess sensitivity causes everything in the test to appear significant.

First, we analyzed the data for normality. The team members started to balk at the time it would take to perform this test—until I showed them how fast the statistical software could complete the test. I also explained that, unless we could be sure that our sample data was normal, we could not make any assumptions based on the mean or standard deviation of the data.

After we determined that our data was indeed normal, we performed tests of equal variance to establish homogeneity of variance. Satisfied with the results, we used T-tests and one-way analysis of variance (ANOVA) to evaluate the means.

Since the inputs to the process did not show any particular problems, it was safe to move to the Improve phase. As we entered that phase, we were somewhat confident that we'd identified the most influential variables.

We next had to evaluate the variables using Design of Experiments (DOE). This is a tool that not only lets us understand the effect of the factors, but also enables us to evaluate the effects of the interactions of the factors. With DOE, you can manipulate all of the variables at the same time, rather than manipulating only one while holding everything else constant, as in the classical approach to experiments.

Black Belts are heavily trained in the statistics behind ANOVA (a DOE technique), but the software did everything that we'd spent days learning. The Black Belts seemed to feel superior in explaining a sophisticated tool—and it sounded very impressive.

The first step in running a successful DOE was to make sure we could measure the factors (x) and the outcome of the factors, the response variable (Y). Since this technique requires setting high and low values, we used the information we'd learned in the Measure phase, so we could separate the various levels of input accurately.

> DOE is a powerful tool that can provide valuable information about process.
> Planning for DOE takes time, but it must be done correctly. If you fail to plan, the process will generate waste with no acceptable learnings from the DOE.

It seems kind of basic, especially since we'd used MSA just a week before, but it was still news to some. I guess changing behavior really does take time and effort. Maybe that equation $Y = (f) x$ applies to change efforts too!

As I make my DOE report notes here, I should warn you: I'm about to talk statistics. You may not be interested. If not, then read ahead. If so, bear with me and I'll make it as painless as possible—but I'll still have to use numbers.

The next step is logistics. What materials do we need? What changes do we need to make to the machine as we change from one group of factors to the next? (This is known as a *treatment combination*.) We designed the experiment with five factors—five inputs that had significant effect on the output characteristic of interest to us.

Since we were going to have five factors at two levels each, there would be 32 treatment combinations (2^5). The team evaluated the cost of running 32 treatment combinations and spoke with our process experts. They were convinced that we would not see any three factors interact in the process.

On that premise, we decided to do what is called a *half-fraction experiment*: we would run only half of the treatment combinations, but we would be able to understand the single-factor effects (known as *main effects*) and we would also be able to understand the two-factor interactions (known as *second-order interactions*).

This is a resolution five design. The use of the half-fraction design also allowed us to do all the treatment combinations twice or to replicate the experiment without incurring excessive costs. This reduced the risk of some random effect creeping into the experiment and causing a factor to look differently than it should.

Once we had selected the design and sample size, we understood how many treatment combinations there would be. If we understood changeover time, then we could calculate how long the experiment would take.

It's important to understand this, because DOEs are intrusive: we will make scrap and it will cost money. The treatment combinations are so prescriptive that the DOE must interfere with production. This was another reason we leveraged the hypothesis testing in the Analyze phase: it was passive in that we collected our data without interfering with the process, so we could do evaluations without interrupting production. This allowed us to enter the DOE planning process with a reasonable number of factors and minimize the interruption.

As we planned the DOE, we also created data sheets for the test lab, so the staff could record all of the data necessary to accurately evaluate the DOE. In addition to the spaces designated for recording required data, there were areas to write down comments and to log anything the team felt might be important. It's better to record too much than to miss something. The team organized all this with very little input from me.

By this point George was getting excited about the possibilities he saw coming out of the experiment. He spent most of his workday involved in the project. As preparations were coming to a close, we assigned people to just observe what was being done and to log anything unusual in the process.

The day before the DOE was scheduled, we conducted a dry run of two treatment combinations. This practice allowed us to do two setups and run everyone through the responsibilities of their positions twice. Everything went well, even though most of the team members were a little nervous. But they felt great—especially Doc.

"Sam, do you have a second?" he asked me as we were all leaving at the close of the day. At first I was worried, but Doc seemed excited.

"Sam, I've got to tell you, I've never felt so valuable to this company." He was smiling broadly. "You remember how I told you that nobody cared what the operator thought about the process? Now people care—and we're making a difference!"

His comment put a smile on my face that lasted for hours. Yes, they were all making a difference.

We cleared up some minor issues with the people who would be involved the next day and moved forward. We ran the DOE and it went relatively smoothly. We got the data in about six hours. The analysis took about 10 minutes, using software designed for that purpose.

I decided to take some of the mystery out of the statistics and conduct the analysis with all team members present. We hooked a laptop computer to an LCD projector and began pointing and clicking. We did the main effects and interaction plots first. They provided basic information in a graphic format. The entire team could see in moments what we had found in the experiment. We discussed what each chart meant. Then we moved on to the ANOVA table.

Ouch! The team members reacted as expected. We saw lots of numbers and acronyms, which had a significant effect, judging from their body language. I immediately began to explain what some of the numbers meant and which ones were there for tradition and really didn't mean anything for our purposes. The more columns of numbers I threw out, the more comfortable they became.

Our data said we'd explained about 78% percent of the total variation. Two main effects and one interaction were significant. The interaction was with one main effect that was significant and the other was not. The next DOE would have to include all three of the factors.

Having weathered the ANOVA table storm, we moved to the residuals—the differences between observations and predictions. This wasn't so bad; I could see the team members becoming more confident as I took the time to present the practical meaning behind each of the numerical outputs they were seeing. The residuals told us we were in good shape: normal and no patterns. We had most of the problem explained.

Then it was time to zero in on the settings for our factors. Getting ready to do our second DOE was much easier. We knew the factors and the measurement systems were the same as in the first DOE. The only thing we were going to change was the level of the factors. We would move them in the direction that gave us the best response. With only three factors, we could do a full factorial, which meant eight treatment combinations. With a replicate (repeat of the experiment), we would run a total of 16.

We ran the DOE the following day, in a little less time than the day before. The analysis was about the same. It turned out we could get to where we want to go using blade design, speed, and the interaction of the two factors.

Frequently this is where the Improve phase ends. But the team recognized that just running the DOE doesn't optimize the process; it only tells you what worked best for the factor levels you used. The next day would be spent on optimization, using evolutionary operation (EVOP) or response surface methodology (RSM).

I explained to the team members that EVOP is a series of linked DOEs, executed in a disciplined manner. The objective is to find the optimal point to run the process.

After every iteration, we assembled the members of the team and they took part in deciding where the next levels would be set.

Doc suggested we "push the envelope" and George agreed.

"Let's not see what we would do under our current process knowledge constraints. Let's really start to understand what this process is capable of."

In the end, the optimal spot was obvious to even the most casual observer. Finally—a solution! And now, the new mixer ....

The most difficult thing at this point was keeping every employee in the facility from wandering by while we were trying to have our team meetings. Michelle was a more positive campaign leader than we'd ever imagined. She had been discussing our success with everyone in the plant and now they all wanted to know when we were going to come help with their processes.

There were still a couple of issues to resolve. As we brought the new mixer into production, we ran the material into the main line. We circled back to the hypothesis testing from the Analyze phase and ran some chi-square tests to compare the number of defects with the old material and the number with the new material. I reminded them that this standard statistical test would show if there was a significant difference between the two levels of defects.

The test indicated we were maintaining the same level of quality on the new mixer as on the old one. We would continue to work on optimizing the two processes later.

The primary objective was for the new mixer to supply the same material as the old mixer. The data showed we'd achieved this goal. We were just about done!

The team worked through the Five S and Standardized Work steps again. Through the Standardized Work training, the team defined the new process as it had been documented and all the operators involved were trained on the new procedures.

Doc volunteered to assist in the training. His enthusiasm sent out a strong message to the rest of the operators. The team also followed up with the training department, so that anyone new to the area would be mentored into the improved process correctly.

Since the quality management system served as an infrastructure for the operation, the procedures were part of the document control system. The laboratory documents were changed as well. All the procedure changes meant these processes would be on the audit schedule for a while, until they had established a record of compliance.

The process engineers had the job of programming the mixer so that many of the parameters were done automatically. What Doc called "just good, common sense" I presented to the team as an example of mistake-proofing or poka-yoke, a Six Sigma approach that reduces the possibility of defects by reducing or eliminating opportunities for error.

Some control charts were put into place in those areas we could not mistake-proof. Everyone understood that control charts require discipline. If any employee didn't intend to comply with maintaining the charts and, more importantly, with shutting down the process when it was out of control, then there was no reason to post the charts. Everyone agreed to proceed with control charting as a measure of improvement in the process.

The next issue was to determine who would create the charts. Quality Assurance had a person who was responsible for creating control charts, so this responsibility was added to her list. The team members would be trained in using and interpreting control charts so they would own that as well.

But they didn't believe we were there yet, there was still one more thing to be done. I was voted to be responsible for this last task. I called Celia and asked her to put the team on the agenda for Sid's staff meeting, to present their accomplishments. I was working with the team to create a 10-minute presentation: this was how Black Belts were taught to present their results and this team had certainly completed a Black Belt project.

I showed up with the team and we waited patiently outside Sid's conference room door until it was time to begin. The door opened and we were ushered in.

While the team was loading its presentation on a computer/projector for the presentation, one of Sid's staff got up from his chair. One of the team members whispered to me, "Look, there goes our controller. He thinks he's above this type of presentation."

On his way out, the controller bent to explain to Sid that we would have to excuse him, because he had something important he needed to do. I immediately felt a hot flash from the top of my head to the tips of my toes. I was getting mad—not for myself but for my team. They deserved better than this.

But before I could utter a word, Sid asked him what was so important that he could not spare 10 or 15 minutes to hear what a team had done to save several hundred thousand dollars for the company. Sid pointed out that he considered it a major function of his staff to attend reviews such as this one.

Sid's message was clear. All of his staff members adjusted their posture. It was equally clear to the project team members that everyone in the room was paying full attention.

The meeting went well. The team members left completely empowered by the experience. They had presented the program as one. No silos of Production, Engineering, Maintenance, etc. They had witnessed Sid communicating his priorities. It was impressive and they felt powerful. They probably wouldn't phrase it quite like that, but they wanted to spread the word—and, most importantly, they wanted to go fix something else.

I love this job! I love being "that guy."

Key Points

- If the correct project is chosen, the Champion will have no problem supporting it, as it will directly impact an important business objective.

- At its heart, Six Sigma is based on statistics. Therefore, the key to any successful Six Sigma implementation is reliable data. The steps taken to reach reliable, acceptable data cannot be skipped or shortened.

Chapter 12

Getting Organized to Get Me Out

*T*he day after the team's presentation, I ran into George in the hall. I glanced his way, ready to give a polite "Hello" and keep moving, since I didn't want to make a big deal out of the success we'd both witnessed.

But the urgency in George's eyes made me stop. My first thought was that he had another pressing problem that he didn't feel quite ready to handle. But George surprised me, *again*.

"Hi, Sam," he said, taking my hand. "Do you remember when you told me you would increase our capacity and margins without any capital outlay or you would walk away from SG?"

I nodded, recalling his skepticism, and I smiled.

"Well," he continued, "you won the bet—but I've decided that I want you out of here … and I want to sit down with you to discuss how we can make that happen."

He paused, then went on to explain.

"The mixer project was so successful that the staff has decided we want to incorporate Lean and Six Sigma into every process in our organization. I have volunteered to be the first name on the roster for our first wave of Black Belt training. And," he concluded, "we want you to help get us through the process."

I accepted George's plan to lay out the transition from dependence to independence, with the understanding that I would be focusing on transferring knowledge and working my way out.

"Sure, Sam," he smiled. "I can't wait to take this through the entire plant."

I called Celia and asked if she could set up a meeting with Sid and George for the next day. Celia said she would arrange it. That meant it would happen.

The meeting was critical for two reasons.

First, we had to establish metrics for the organization. At present, they were keeping track of the wrong things.

A good example was hours on the job. There was an engineering supervisor who stood at the plant exit every day at the end of first shift and wrote down names of the engineering staff who left after eight hours. Every time I saw him standing there, I wondered if he considered this value-added work. It was amazing that he considered it work at all.

One of the things I was planning to explain to Sid was that *time* at the job didn't correlate to *accomplishment* on the job. If I could get the management group focused on the correct metrics, they would no longer waste time wondering who was working the longest hours.

> *Time* on the job isn't the same as *accomplishment* on the job. Just showing up doesn't add value.

The other reason I wanted to meet with Sid and George was that they had displayed some very good behaviors recently. Just like the team, it was important that they receive some positive reinforcement for the good things, just in case they were having trouble distinguishing between the good and the bad.

The project stuff is the most fun for a plant rat like me. The most important thing I could do for the operations people was not to work projects, but to try to guide the company leaders toward more productive behaviors.

The next morning I checked my voice mail. Celia had left me a message that the meeting I had requested was scheduled for noon. It would be a working lunch for Sid. I decided to eat after the meeting; it would be better if I focused on talking.

I arrived at noon and Celia showed me in. I thanked her for arranging the meeting. Sid and George were unwrapping their lunches. Both thanked me for the work I had done with the team.

The thought came to me that they had no idea how far this Lean Six Sigma initiative would take them. They were pleased with the success so far, because it had made the plant more efficient. But how would they feel when Lean Six Sigma extended into operations beyond the plant, into their own offices?

I had observed over time that residents of the white-collar world believed that Lean Six Sigma programs were geared toward manufacturing. Transactional processes, since they occur in offices, must be different.

It was truly amazing that everyone struggled with applying these concepts outside of manufacturing. As one of "those guys," I've found that all organizations have one thing in common—their unyielding belief that they are *different!* The truth of the matter is that the differences between manufacturing and transactional problems are negligible. Rather than wasting time searching for those differences, we should be working to understand the similarities.

But I digress ....

Sid and George spent about 10 minutes talking about how well the Lean and Six Sigma programs were going. They enjoyed the presentation by the project team members because it had clearly demonstrated that if we had focused on the defect level alone the mixer would still be an issue and we still would not know it.

We spent the next half hour or so discussing the many things they'd been doing that were helping to make the Lean and Six Sigma programs successful. They'd had a couple of successes that they could publicize around the plant so people would understand what was going on. I reminded them of a point that they should make clear, the fact highlighted in the presentation that organizations don't have to choose between Lean and Six Sigma and that the two tools should never be perceived as mutually exclusive.

Further, I explained that their job as managers was to lead the integration and drive the alignment with company vision and mission statements. I handed them a couple of pages I'd created to help them understand what I was talking about.

The first page, Basic Flow: Lean Six Sigma Integration Model, showed the links among several pieces of the initiative puzzle and how they need to fit together. Sid and George both thought this was interesting, but it lacked detail. If they were going to implement successfully, they needed more detail.

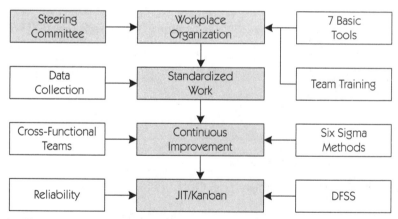

Basic Flow: Lean Six Sigma Integration Model

I explained how I did not intend to give them a cookbook. The "one size fits all" mentality was not appropriate here. The details for deployment and integration should come from the steering committee. It is *that* detailed plan that allows them to understand when and where they can use a consultant. More importantly, the work of the committee will help to control the time and involvement of that consultant, so "that guy" won't still be there 10 years from now working on implementation.

The next page of the handout provided the same structure, a block diagram, but this one covered the involvement of the steering committee. Before reviewing this next page, I did a sanity check with Sid and George to make sure we were all still on the same page (literally). Both said they weren't positive they had all the links, but they felt pretty comfortable continuing the discussion, so we moved on to the second chart, "Steering Committee: Inputs and Outputs."

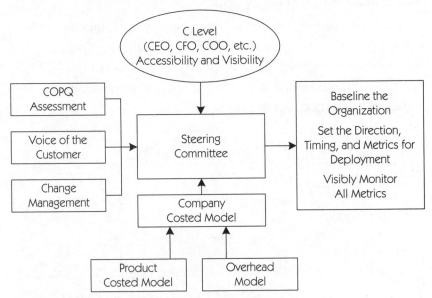

Steering Committee: Inputs and Outputs

They now understood that the steering committee had to have input from all areas of the business before it could produce the baseline, deployment plan, and metrics. Surprisingly, Sid and George were right on board when I explained that we were right back at the problem-solving model, $Y = (f) x$. The problem seems so much simpler when you understand the relationship between dependent and independent variables. Effective change happens only when we understand the independent variables.

The next chart—"Six Sigma Basic Integration Model"—defined what would be necessary in order to implement a comprehensive Six Sigma program. Both Sid and George's eyes were beginning to glaze over. I told them not to worry—this stuff is always difficult to comprehend all at once. I suggested they introduce the idea at the next staff meeting and see what the reaction was. It would be Sid's job to orchestrate the overall strategy.

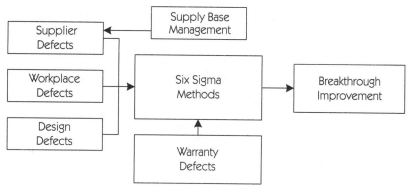

Six Sigma Basic Integration Model

I went on to explain that, since George had been the beneficiary of a lot of the improvement, he should be involved in selling the concept. Both nodded as if they understood.

We adjourned and I excused myself, leaving Sid and George pondering the charts I had just given them. My final recommendation in the meeting was to consider putting Michelle in the role of facilitator for the training we were about to undertake.

One thing was sure: both men understood that my main priority was to make SG, Inc. independent. And they knew that, although they had a long way to go, they were on the right path.

On my way back to my workspace, I stopped again and thanked Celia for setting up the meeting for me. I knew that we would need her organizational talent to pull off all the training ahead. But SG, Inc. was definitely making great progress!

Key Points

- The most important thing a consultant can do for operations is not to work projects, but to try to guide the company leaders toward more productive behaviors.

- Lean and Six Sigma apply to all operations, whether manufacturing or transactional. The differences between problems in those areas are negligible.

Index

About the Authors

Barbara Wheat is the Director of Six Sigma for Ingersoll-Rand Tool and Hoist Division, where she brings the tools and techniques of both Lean Enterprise and Six Sigma together to institutionalize a world-class system of continuous improvement.

Chuck Mills has taught and implemented Lean Enterprise tools and techniques to forward-thinking organizations in both the United States and Europe.

Mike Carnell is President of Six Sigma Applications, one of the oldest and most experienced Six Sigma providers.